Cover picture is Adolph Rupp drawing a "guard-around" play

1

Table of Contents

Introduction

Ours was a sports-oriented family of five boys and two girls born to Russell Ganes Rice and Alpha Bowe Rice in Johnson County, Ky., and reared during the Great Depression. Our father began working in the Van Lear coal mines at age fourteen. He lied about his age; Consol needed workers for the five mines the company then operated up and down Millers Creek.

A mine foreman taught my father the multiplication tables on pieces of slate by carbide light, deep inside the mines. Ganes eventually became a union secretary and for his own satisfaction, a keeper of UK statistics. His sons inherited their father's love of sports.

I earned letters in three sports at Van Lear High School and played briefly on the Kentucky Wesleyan baseball team. Brother Randy and I often took turns announcing imaginary UK games. Brother Jim played on the Garrett High School team that lost to Shelbyville in the 1948 KHSAA basketball tournament. Brother Clarence Darrell was captain of his Pikeville College basketball team. He later coached basketball at the middle and high school levels. Brother Bob still plays pick-up games at the Indianapolis, Ind., YMCA.

I was four years old when our father brought home two BIG batteries and a radio to our non-electric home in Wittensville. Those two items were a wagon-load. He attached a radio antenna to the tallest tree on the hill behind our house. It pulled in much static. That was seven years before WLAP-Radio in Lexington aired UK's first basketball game vs. Xavier in 1935.

We soon moved to Van Lear. We would gather around the radio and listen to prize fights, Lum & Abner, and church music. We welcomed the arrival of the Grand Old Opry and high school basketball on the airways.

I was a 5-foot-8 ½ inch, 150 pound center/linebacker on our football team. I started most of the time, not because I was a

4

good player, but due to a lack of depth on our team. Of the 18 students in our senior class (1942) there were only nine boys. When the United States entered WW-II, we voted on whether to field a football team that year. Two of us voted to continue playing the game, which was certainly unrealistic.

The company constructed a football field in the lower end of Van Lear, near the Levisa Fork of the Big Sandy River. It was approximately 1½ miles from the gymnasium. That was a long walk after a hard scrimmage session. Practically no one owned a car.

The C&O railroad and the main highway bordered one side, and Millers Creek on the other side of the field. A set of bleachers sat at one end behind what served as home plate during baseball games. The other end consisted of a corn field. The only room (standing) for spectators, other than the baseball bleachers, was on the railroad side of the field.

Due to poor roads and restricted travel, we played practically all our games close to home. That meant regular series with Inez, Meade Memorial, Paintsville, Prestonsburg, Jenkins and Pikeville, and occasional games with Kermit and Chattaroy, W.Va. We didn't win many of those games.

Van Lear once had a proud football tradition. That was prior to the 1940s, before the five coal mines began playing out. When I was growing up, the town had a population of 4,000, largest in the county. However, with the area's population diminishing and war clouds looming, we said goodbye to football and hello to basketball.

The first basketball game that I saw was a loss to Paintsville on a muddy court in the corner of our schoolyard. Spectators stood on the sidewalk that split the yard and continued uphill to the school.

In 1935, the Works Progress Administration (WPA) constructed a gym across the creek from our home. When not involved in school, gardening, or other chores, I eagerly watched the gym go up.

Two rooms flanked a stage on one side of the gym playing floor. Participating teams occupied benches at their perspective ends of the stage. Substitutes climbed up and down the stage. There was a large coal-burning stove located on each end of the bleachers on the other side of the floor. Those two monsters emitted enough heat to roast persons nearest them. The back-rows spectators wore extra clothing, usually sheepskin jackets. . Although warmer than the others in attendance, those persons nearest the stoves also had to dodge tobacco juice sailing overhead and spewing onto the stoves. Most men chewed tobacco, many smoked roll-your-own cigarettes in those days.

Our love affair with the Wildcats began when we finally were able to get their games on the radio. The Ashland Daily Independent kept us informed of the antics of Wallace Jones and other UK stars during the "Fabulous Five" era.

I was just out of the Marine Corps in 1946 when UK freshman guard Ralph Beard sank a free throw that gave UK a 46-45 win over Rhode Island in the 1946 NIT championship game. I turned off the radio and had my best night's sleep in years.

(This introduction is from The Big Blue Nation: Kentucky Basketball's Native Sons and Daughters, by Russell Rice, Still Publications, Eubank, KY, 2011. The cover design and formatting were done by Danny Breeden and his son Sean; both are computer whizzes).

Chapter One
Tradition

"My genuine opinion of the Kentucky basketball program is that there is only one and it is top drawer, Park Avenue, and that all other basketball programs in the country think they are, but they are not. The closest ones to get to it (Kentucky) are North Carolina, maybe Indiana, and UCLA. But at Kentucky, basketball is a type of religion, such a fanatical obsession that they expect to be national champion each year, and they live and die with each ball game."

—Al McGuire, foreword to Joe B. Hall, My Own Kentucky Home.

Al McGuire said he was not looking to throw a party for Kentucky, but was merely expressing his feelings. He considered his an honest appraisal because he'd seen all the programs, as a coach, a player, and as an NBC commentator. "I have touched all the so-called capitals of basketball," McGuire said, "but when it gets down to the short stroke the only true capital of basketball is Lexington"

Lonnie Wheeler, in his book, Blue Yonder, explores the "mysterious culture" that is Kentucky basketball. He writes of "a memorial odyssey that navigates the thick-bloodied hollows of Appalachia, the colonial monarchy of Adolph Rupp, the ignominies of point-shaving and probation, the racial traditions that have stigmatized a sacred institution, the momentous responses of a cutting edge coach, and the inscrutable partnership of country people who sue their siblings over inherited tickets, call in death threats to critical reporters, and get buried with blue and white pom-poms in their caskets."

Wheeler is one of the many authors who have elevated UK basketball to the top of books and articles about its storied program. Coaches, staff members, professors, players, managers, team doctors, media types, roommates and fans have become published authors, all pursuing the underlying theme that in

Kentucky basketball is king. Ralph Beard appeared on the first cover of Sports Illustrated in 1948. The magazine has featured the Wildcats on nineteen of its covers. Kentucky's leading newspapers and Sporting News are among those who have published books about UK's championship teams. The nation's largest media contingent follows the Cats; Media Relations issues upward of 100 media passes for games in Rupp Arena.

Kentucky leads the nation in home basketball attendance yearly, and its following of fans is legendary. When the Wildcats played in the 1997 Maui Classic, more than 1,000 fans joined them in Hawaii. They purchased every ticket available in the cramped gym (2,500 capacity), filling an entire side with Blue. In 2004 they helped set a world-record attendance of 78,129 in a victory over Michigan State in Detroit. Every other year since 1985, Kentucky fans have played games in Freedom Hall. More than 20,000 UK fans filled the stands for those games. The same is true in Cincinnati, where Wildcat fans outdraw the hometown favorite local teams with more than 16,000 blue-clad supporters in U.S. Bank One arena on an alternating basis. From 1988-2006, UK played Indiana in Louisville and Indianapolis. More than 40,000 fans in the RCA Dome created one of college basketball's most visible events. The series ended in 2012 after four years on a home-to-home basis.

Basketball succeeded in Kentucky partly because of the essentially rural nature of the state. Any hamlet large or small could afford a sport that equipped its players in scant uniforms, and needing only a ball, a couple of hoops, and a place to play. The early high schools played their state tournaments on the UK campus. They played a major role in elevating the sport and the Wildcats to an exalted status.

However, basketball in Kentucky is more than a rural game; it encompasses cities and towns of all sizes. Wildcat basketball knows no bounds; it attracts fans of all colors and creeds, at home and abroad.

Early Wildcat rosters consisted mostly of Kentucky natives. That was due mainly to travel restrictions and the economics of the times. High school games provided a rallying point for communities throughout the state. Lexington soon becomes a Mecca of college basketball.

"When a Kentucky baby is born, the mother naturally wants him to be president, like another Kentuckian, Abraham Lincoln," Adolph Rupp said. "If not president, she wants him to play basketball for the University of Kentucky."

Rupp eventually extended his recruiting range into Indiana and Ohio. The Big Ten coaches accused him of being a carpetbagger. Five native Kentuckians—Ralph Beard, Joe Holland, Wallace Jones, Kenny Rollins and Jack Tingle—made the 1947 All-Conference team.

No matter the makeup of a team, local or otherwise, black or white, Wildcat fans roll with the flow, so to speak, and embrace all wearers of the Blue & White. The players return in kind by continuing the steady flow of championships and All-Americans.

"It's been said ad infinitum that being a basketball fan in Kentucky is a lifelong occupation," Pat Forde wrote is A Legacy of Champions. "Now we know that's incorrect. It's longer than that. Why wait to start at birth? A few years ago one Kentucky fan mailed an ultrasound of his unborn baby to coach Rick Pitino, for storage in his future recruiting files."

In 1991, they buried a man from Pikeville with a card from mountain hero John Pelphrey in his casket. An elderly woman was interned with a UK basketball by her side. An autographed picture of the 1948 Wildcats accompanied another fan to the grave. A Hopkinsville widow left the team $42,000. A grandmother in Falmouth filled an icebox with notebooks of scores of every UK game for 45 years.

Simeon Hale, who was in his 90's, rode a bus approximately 100 miles from Pulaski County in rural Southeastern Kentucky to attend UK home games. Although he had a crippled leg, Hale walked from his place in the country to a road where he flagged a bus to Somerset. Then he caught a bus to Lexington. He took a nap at the bus station until time for the game. He walked back to the station after the game, slept on a bench there until three o'clock in the morning, when he rode a bus back to Somerset, a 24-hour ordeal.

In the early 1930s, WLAP aired Lexington's first sports radio program. The format featured interviews with the Kentucky football coach and coaches of the upcoming opponents.

The **Graves-Cox Co.***, Lexington's leading men's clothing store, sponsored the program. Paul Nickell, a star salesman for the firm, convinced his friend, Adolph Rupp, the youthful Wildcat basketball coach, to serve as the interviewer.*

In lieu of pay, Nickell outfitted Rupp in the company's most expensive brown suit and matching accessories: brown hat, brown shirt, brown shoes, brown socks, and a brown tie. Rupp also did commentary for the station during KHSAA State Tournament games held in Alumni Gym.

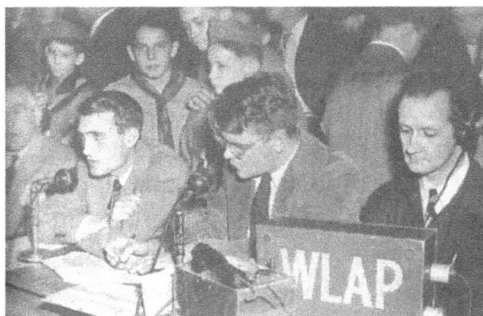

Kyle Macy said UK was the only major college team with a tremendous following all over the state. "When I was at Purdue, the state of Indiana was about evenly divided in its loyalty among Purdue, Indiana, and Notre Dame," he said. "Where else but at Kentucky could a player get 100 to 200 letters a week from fans? Where else could a player have babies named after him?"

Fans write poems and sing songs about the Wildcats. They bake cakes and cookies. They remember players' birthdays.

Legislators introduce resolutions praising them, governors and mayors declare days in their honor.

Pomp and pageantry play a major role in the Wildcat mystique. "Senior Day" is a season-ending celebration. It begins with class members bursting through banners bearing their likenesses and meeting family members at center court. Then everyone joins in singing "My Old Kentucky Home." The lowest senior reserve gets a chance to start the last home game of the year.

"Basketball in Kentucky gives the populace something to put on a pedestal." Pat Forde wrote. "In Kentucky, basketball players are our royalty. Cawood Ledford, in addition to near-flawless with his call of the game, was a UK fan's' key to the mythical kingdom."

Kentucky Hoops on the airwaves

Tom Leach and Mike Pratt

For the past seven decades, Kentucky basketball radio broadcasts have been a unifying force in a state divided into four diverse sections. From the mountains to the east, to the Purchase in the west, to the urban north, and to the rural south, a Wildcat radiocast is an event that many residents rate next to the Kentucky Derby. Al McGuire wrote in Inside Sports, "The kids in Kentucky start listening to the games on the radio when they are still being burped on their father's shoulder"

But, before radio, there was the teletype. When Kentucky played Georgia, in the 1921 championship game of the SIAA Tournament in Atlanta, UK students and fans gathered on a balcony at Lexington's Phoenix Hotel. A telegraph operator stood by to receive news of the game. Shortly before tip-off, Albert E. Hukle, flushed face matching his red hair, stretched his slender, 6-fooot-5 frame, looked down at the crowded lobby, took a deep breath, raised a megaphone, and read the first message:

"Game ready to start. Boys in fine shape." The final buzzer sounded with the score tied, 19-19, and Kentucky's William King on the free-throw line. The telegraph keys clicked the following message: "King scores one point. Final score Kentucky 20 Georgia 19. Bring home cup tomorrow. Greatest game ever played."

The 1921 SIAA Tournament Champion Wildcats (front l to r) are Sam Ridgeway, Paul Adkins, Basil Hayden, Bill King, and Bobby Lavin; (back) Coach George Buchheit, Jim Wilhelm, Bill Poynz, Gilbert Smith and AD S.A. Boles

Exuberant fans shoulder-carried the team members from the Lexington railway station to the Phoenix Hotel. They attended a banquet was held in honor of the "First Basketball Champions of the South".

The first live radio broadcast of a Kentucky basketball game was held March 7, 1935, at the season finale against

Xavier in Alumni Gym. Earlier that season several simulated accounts of out-of-town games were broadcast from the studios of WLAP.

Eddie Sutton Happy Chandler singing My Old Kentucky Home

Sportswriter Ed Ashford re-created the play-by-play from wire reports while an engineer provided sound effects. The state high school tournament also was broadcast for the first time that year. Adolph Rupp and Happy Chandler assisted Ashford on the microphone.

J. B. Faulconer joined WLAP in 1939 after serving as senior manager of the Wildcat basketball team. He broadcast for the first time in 1940, doing football and not basketball. After returning from the army in 1946, Faulconer became the station's sports director. He worked the UK basketball and football games.

In the early days of radio broadcasts, fans in eastern Kentucky drove atop the highest mountain to tune in the Wildcat games. Transplanted Kentuckians in Dayton and Detroit drove the city blocks seeking a signal from Louisville's WHAS, a 50,000-watt station that carried the UK games.

A pilot flying his route over Kentucky late one night commented about all the houses being lit up beneath his plane.

The explanation was simple: the radios were tuned to a Wildcat basketball game. If they remained on afterward, it meant the Wildcats had lost the game.

An Iowa man was known as "Tombstone Johnny' because he operated a tombstone business in the Hawkeye state. The impact of listening to games via radio made him a UK fan. Johnny attended some UK games played in the Midwest.

Cawood's Corner in Rupp Arena

Johnny T. drove 775 miles from Iowa to watch games in Rupp Arena. "Tombstone" Johnny eventually enrolled his son in UK and moved his family to Lexington.

Dr. V. A. Jackson gave up a profitable medical practice in western Kentucky and moved to Lexington in order to be near the Wildcats. He eventually became one of the team's doctors. Once he treated a man for terminal cancer who wouldn't take his morphine because he wanted a clear head when he listened to radio broadcasts of UK games.

A family in Pikeville sat a six-year-old son on the dining room table with his feet crossed Indian style during UK games. When a Kentucky player shot a free throw, they all rubbed his head for good luck.

Ashland Oil and WHAS formed a network that sometimes had as many as 40 stations, depending on whom they played. During the post WWII years, Lexington stations WLAP, WVLK, WLEX and WBKY and WHAS carried the UK games. Claude Sullivan became a favored "Voice" at WVLK before dying of throat cancer in 1967.

Phil Sutterfield reached a large audience through WHAS (50,000 watts) and its network affiliates. He also conducted Bear Bryant's popular radio shows.

These radio personalities opened the doors of UK's mythical basketball kingdom. They were affectionately known as the "Voices of the Wildcats". Standing tallest among those was Cawood Ledford, who did play-by-play of both Wildcat basketball and football games for 39 years (1953-1992).

In 1953, newly established WLEX hired Cawood Ledford as a sports commentator. On Sept. 10, Ledford worked his first UK game, a football loss to Texas A&M. By the sixth game, the station promoted him to play-by-play announcer. Three years later, Ledford joined the sports team at WHAS in Louisville.

Ledford became a legend in his own time, thanks to UK's championship teams. When he walked onto the playing floor of Rupp Arena, the students would chant, "Hello Cawood!" He would wave to the crowd.

Kentucky held a farewell dinner in Rupp Arena for Cawood. It raised $135,000 for a scholarship named in his honor. The fund is intended to help athletes work on their degrees after their eligibility expires. Cawood's retired jersey hangs among others in the rafters of Rupp Arena.

After Claude Sullivan's death, his wife Alyce kept the network together for one year before UK sold its broadcast

The G. H. Johnston Agency of New York City entered the high bid and retained Ledford as its play-by-play announcer. Ledford left WHAS that year (1968) and joined with Jim Host to form Cawood Ledford Productions. Host is a UK baseball letterman who worked radio broadcasts of some UK games in the early 1960s, when four radio broadcast teams traveled with the Wildcats.

Ralph Hacker was another well-known "voice of the Wildcats". Hacker was the "voice" of the basketball Wildcats for nine years and did the play-by-play for Kentucky football for five seasons. Hacker and Ledford became known as one of the nation's premier collegiate broadcasting teams for 20 years. Hacker retired prior to the 2001-2002 season. Tom Leach and Mike Pratt form the current UK broadcast team.

In 1974 Jim Host & Associates entered the high bid for UK sports broadcast rights. Host has been a major figure in UK sports broadcasts since that time. It has held similar contracts with UK in all but six years since 1974. Jim Host is no longer affiliated with Host Communications.

Host built a network with 125 stations in Kentucky, Indiana, Ohio, Tennessee, West Virginia, and Florida. One survey found that UK games could be heard in forty states as well as Canada and the Bahamas. Host later served as Kentucky's secretary of commerce.

In October, 2004, the university awarded Host Communications Inc. and Gray Television Inc. expanded athletic multimedia marketing rights. Host teamed up with Lexington's top-rated television station, WKYT-TV, to pay the university $80,745,000 over the 10 years of the agreement, making it one of the most lucrative deals of its kind in NCAA history.

Wildcats on Television

The University of Kentucky basketball team's first television appearance occurred in the 1951 NCAA eastern finals when their wins over St. John's and Illinois were televised nationally from Madison Square Garden. As part of a salute to Coach Rupp, the Tonight Show aired portions of a UK game with Loyola in Chicago Stadium on Feb. 15. 1957.

NBC's "Game of the Week" series in 1958/59 featured UK wins over St. Louis, LSU, and Tennessee. An ABC-TV series in 1961 aired UK's win over Georgia Tech in Memorial Coliseum.

16

During that era, a young law school graduate named Eddie Einhorn founded TVS Television Network. It became the leading syndicate of sports program in the 1970's, which helped give rise to the popularity of college basketball on television.

When Einhorn televised UK's 1962 game with Georgia Tech in Atlanta, UK urged its fans to send in donations, even if just for a dollar, to help pay for the transmission. Since those "pioneer" days, the Wildcats have become regulars on coast-to-coast telecasts. In addition to the SEC series, ESPN, Fox, and other networks, the university created its own TV network, which airs on a delayed basis games not otherwise televised.

Since 1991, nearly every UK game has been televised—nationally, regionally, or statewide. During the 2003-04 season, every game was televised either live or delayed. UK appeared on national television in 17 of its 32 games.

In 20004/05, Rob Bromley entered his 25th year on the UK Television Network, handling play-by-play duties for live and delayed broadcasts. Martin Newman joined the network as broadcast analyst in 1994/95. Dave Baker, pre-game host, and Dick Gabriel, sideline reporter, are the veteran members of the team.

Midnight Madness

Dirk Minnifield

17

Kentucky moved its Midnight Madness into Rupp Arena in 2005, dispensing 23,000 tickets in less than one hour. That was almost three times more than the 8,500+ that attended the initial session in October, 1982. That first Madness consisted of an introduction of the coaches and players, some routine drills and the shooting of lay-ups.

The late Steve Rardin, a news distributor in Lexington, set the record of attending 627 consecutive UK basketball games. He ended an earlier streak Dec. 31, 1968, when he attended a family wedding while the Wildcats lost to Wisconsin in Chicago Stadium.

Rick Pitino met Rardin soon after arriving in Lexington. The Wildcats opened that 1989/90 season with a win over Ohio at home. Then they traveled to Indianapolis and lost by two points to the Hoosiers. Rardin became ill during the game and was hospitalized. Pitino visited him two days before he died.

Bob Wiggins

Ten thousand fans showed up the following year to watch a highly rated team led by Sam Bowie, Melvin Turpin and Kenny Walker. Four years later, more than 12,500 fans were crowded inside the Coliseum by 9:50 p.m. The fire marshal closed the doors, leaving hundreds stranded outside.

The events carried such themes as "Big Blue New Year," "Rockin' after Midnight," "Late Night with the Cats," and "Monster Mash," to name a few before evolving into what is now termed "Big Blue Special." The introduction of new recruits is always accompanied by thundering ovations.

A 1993 event highlight featured Bill "Mr. Wildcat" Keightley emerging from a cake celebrating the program's 100th birthday. The 1995 Madness saw Walter McCarty and Tony Delk swoop down on ropes from high above, dressed like Batman and Robin.

Bob Wiggins, a retired engineer from Falmouth, 50 miles north of Lexington, attended his first UK basketball game in 1944. At one point he witnessed 615 consecutive games. That streak ended when a heart problem prevented him from attending the Great Alaska Shoot in November 1996. The last time Wiggins missed a game before then was back in 1961 when a nine-inch snowfall forced him to turn back at Paris, Ky., only a couple dozen miles from Lexington.

The department passed out tickets five days before an event; lines of students encircle the Coliseum. In 1996, Wally Clark stationed himself by the front door, a full 38 days before the "Back to Tradition" celebration.

Clayton Cregger became a UK fan in 1970. He's been attending Madness since the early 1990s, an annual trek of 292 miles that began when he wrote then-coach Rick Pitino a welcome-to-UK letter. An outgoing man with an irrepressible spirit, Cregger included a request for Madness tickets in his letter. To his surprise, Cregger got a return call a few days later that included instructions on how to pick up Madness tickets at the Coliseum's will-call window. Since then, he's driven to Lexington every year to attend Madness.

A big part of Midnight Madness is the "spirit teams" that follow the hoops team.

The UK cheerleading squad was once billed as a perfect complement to the school's championship-caliber basketball teams. During two decades beginning in 1985, they won 12

Universal Cheerleading Association championships, including eight in a row during one stretch. Since live wildcats seldom thrive in captivity, the university introduced a costumed Wildcat during the 1977/78 season. Wildcat now has a sidekick, Scratch, who joined the cheerleading squad in the mid '90s in conjunction with the UK Kids' Club. Their popularity extends beyond the sports arenas and includes appearances at charity functions, mall openings and many other such events.

The UK Dance Team performs at halftime of all home basketball and football games. In 2003, the squad finished third in the USA College Dance Team Nationals at Las Vegas. The 1996 dancers appeared each week nationally on Monday Night Football, performing during the game's opening with Hank Williams, Jr. Also performing at UK games is an 80-member Pep Band, described by Southern Living magazine as one of the "top ten bands in the South"

Chapter Two
The Arenas

Kentucky basketball teams have played in various venues throughout the state and the country. Their first "home court" was the Barker Hall Armory and their most recent home court is Rupp Arena, a modern coliseum that is packed during Wildcat games.

Barker Hall
(The Armory)

The arrival of William Walter H. Mustaine as the newly appointed physical director at the University of Kentucky in the fall of 1902 coincided with the dedication of newly completed Alumni Hall (later to become known as Barker Hall). It was a three-story structure high in the center with lower wings on each side. The south wing housed Buell Armory, where cadets drilled on a dirt floor. The school annual described it as "a splendid room with a good floor, an elevated running track and all the apparatus necessary for complete gymnastic training."

*The women's gym in Barker Hall was home to the boys' team
during the early days of UK basketball*

In January 1903, Mustaine met with a small group of
students interested in the game of basketball. "I remember
chipping in my quarter to help buy the ball, which cost three
dollars," said Thomson R. "Tommie" Bryant, who had just
turned 90 in January of 1975. "It was one of those you inflated
with a foot pump and then laced."

The manager scheduled UK's first game at home with
Georgetown College, which is located only a few miles north of
Lexington. State trailed the visitors, 7-1, at halftime, and lost the
game, 15-6, or 17-6, according to which newspaper account one
chooses to believe. The gym was packed with rooters for the two
teams who continually applauded the "brilliant plays" of their
respective colleges. All those present considered the game a
rousing success, a very interesting event with both teams giving
an excellent exhibition of basketball.

The Wildcats finished that first season with an 11-10 win
over the local YMCA and a 42-2 loss to KU. They won only
three of 13 games played the following three years, but the game
itself was fast becoming the center of interest in the Lexington
area. The Wildcats needed a better facility and a full-time coach
to accompany this enthusiasm.

The school rated basketball a second cousin to debate
teams and a distant cousin to football. Dr. H. H. Downing, a
retired professor of astronomy at UK, jumped center for the

22

Cadets in 1908. He recalled many years later that there was little student and no off-campus interest in basketball at the time.

The school newspaper reported later that the students took practically no interest in basketball during its first seven years at the school, and that the sport lost money. The basketball team also suffered from lack of practice time in a gym that was overloaded with activities. The situation became so acute that the Faculty Committee on Athletics in November 1909 passed a resolution abolishing the game of basketball as a varsity sport at the university.

This 1904 photo from Kentucky's second season of basketball is one of the earliest known: (left to right) R. H. Arnett, J. White Guyn, Joe Coons, C. P. St John, H. J. Wurtele, and H. H. Downing with the ball

The Kentucky Gazette said the cause of the action was a view that things are better never done than half done. The gymnasium building had become so overcrowded with the required work that there was absolutely no time for the basketball team to practice. Since the matter had been threshed over and over again with no solution, the faculty decided the best way out of the difficulty was to do away with the sport entirely.

The committee rescinded the resolution after they floored the armory in early December.

The university played their home games in Woodland Auditorium in 1916, which is still credited as part of the Armory period. During those years, the Wildcat's compiled a record of 134-108-1. The tie game was played against Kentucky Wesleyan at Winchester in 1918. It resulted from a scorer's error that was not discovered until after the game, which they never re-scheduled.

The Wildcats experienced an undefeated (9-0) season in 1910 and were 13-1 in 1921 after winning the first Southern Intercollegiate Athletic Association (SIAA) tournament at Atlanta. Winning that first "Basketball Championship of the South" sparked a demand for a new basketball arena to keep pace with the ever-increasing popularity of basketball at the university.

Alumni Gym

Kentucky closed out its tenure at Alumni Gym with 84 consecutive victories. The gym still stands at the corner of South Limestone and Avenue of Champions.

In 1923, the UK Alumni Association raised $100,000 toward purchase of a new 2,800-seat facility to accommodate the growing demands of basketball and to assure continuation of the popular state high school tournament on the campus. They located the new building, aptly named Alumni Gymnasium, on Winslow Street, west of the football stadium. Skeptics called it a "white elephant."

Wildcat teams compiled a 247-24 record during the 26 years—1924/25-1949-50-- that they called Alumni Gym their home.

When Adolph Rupp took over the program in 1930/31, the Wildcats established a home record of 201 victories and only eight losses in 19 seasons. Their streak of 84 consecutive wins in the gym included 64 consecutive victories in the Southeastern Conference.

The most home games a UK team lost in a season at Alumni Gym was eight of 10 games played there in 1927. There were three seasons when they lost two games, 10 seasons with one loss each, and 10 non-losing home seasons. They suffered only one losing season in that era.

During their last 17 seasons in the Alumni Gym era, the Wildcats won two NCAA titles, an NIT championship, 12 conference tournament crowns and three Sugar Bowl championships. The demand for tickets became so great that only a portion of the student body and faculty gained admittance to the games. There were no seats available for the general public.

Because the need for a modern facility with more seats, better lighting, and current technologies, Alumni Gym outgrew its size and a new arena was to be built. However, the thought of losing the final game played in Alumni Gym and of losing the streak of 84 home victories preyed heavily on Rupp's mind as his team trailed Vanderbilt by 12 points halftime of the last game played in the old gym.

"Boys, a man spends a lifetime compiling a record, and in one given night a bunch of bums like you are about to tear it down," he told his team at halftime. "If it looks like we're going to go down in defeat tonight, I want you to know that I am personally going to do something to this facility before the game is over and before you get out of this gym." Kentucky won the game, 70-66.

With that victory, Alumni Gym and Rupp's legacy in it were retired.

Memorial Coliseum

The University of Kentucky dedicated its new basketball field house during Commencement Week in the spring of 1951. Named in memory of Kentuckians killed in World War II, the multipurpose facility was constructed at a cost of $4,000,000. Classically simple in design, the facility contains as much space as a seven-story office building covering an entire block. In addition to a basketball arena seating 11,500 persons, it contained a complete plant for the teaching of physical education.

Memorial Coliseum was built in 1950 and stands as a tribute to those Kentuckians who lost their lives in WWII and the Korean War.

Although some skeptics deemed the Coliseum a white elephant, Rupp called it the Taj Mahal of basketball arenas. "Those soreheads are probably the same people who said the same thing about Alumni Gym." Rupp said. "We outgrew that old place real quick."

Contrary to public opinion, the new arena was not filled to capacity from the beginning; all the seats, especially the fold-outs on each side of the court, were not in place. However, the 8,000 fans who witnessed an opening 73-43 victory over West Texas State represented the second largest crowd ever to see a basketball game in Kentucky.

The seats were in place and a capacity crowd was in attendance Dec. 9, when the Cats officially dedicated the Coliseum with a 70-52 win over Purdue. UK vice president Leon M. Chamberlain urged that the building be the home of true sportsmanship, and the source of men of exalted minds, of vigorous bodies, and of great character.

On Jan. 24, 1970, UK students turned out en mass for a game between the Wildcats and an LSU team that featured "Pistol" Pete Maravich. The university seated them in the aisles and on the floor. When the Fire Marshal said enough is enough, a total of 13,690 bodies filled a building with a seating capacity of 11,500. UK won the game, 109-96.

The Wildcats won every game played in the building for the first three seasons. When Georgia Tech upset them, 59-58, on Jan. 8, 1955, it marked the first time in 12 years the Wildcats had lost on their home court. The loss also ended a national streak of 129 straight home wins, which still stands today.

In 26 years, only 25 seasons as the NCAA suspended UK from play in 1952/53, the Wildcats compiled a record of 306-38 in the Coliseum. Since the reign of "King Cotton" Nash, 1962-64, basketball season ticket sales were closed to the general public; only season ticket holders, students and staff were assured admittance to the games.

The building still houses the UK Athletic Association offices and is home to many Wildcat athletic teams. It seats 8,300 spectators.

Rupp Arena (1977-Present)

When Adolph Rupp first stepped into the basketball palace that bears his name, he gawked, shook his head, and said, "My Gawd. It's BIG!" The Baron wasn't exaggerating. Built by the City of Lexington, the arena is the major portion of a 53 million Lexington Center complex that includes a convention-exhibition hall, a 50-store tri-level, enclosed shopping mall and a luxury Hyatt Regency Hotel. Developers Don and Dudley Webb, avid UK fans, built an adjoining Radisson hotel as part of a package that lured the 1985 Final Four to Lexington.

Rupp Arena

The arena is fully air-conditioned, equipped with a specially designed high-quality sound system, and state-of-the-art lighting for events and television coverage. The awesome structure contains two seating areas—a lower level featuring 10,000 cushioned theater seats and an upper level of 13,000 seats on epoxy-coated metal bleachers. It even had its own museum.

The University of Kentucky Basketball Museum, which opened its doors to the public in 1999, provided fans an opportunity to indulge in "Big Blue Fever." Located in Rupp Arena, it featured such attractions as an All-American gallery and a virtual court that allowed fans to play one-on-one against their favorite Wildcats.

One section contained replicas of UK's NCAA trophies, while irreplaceable memorabilia was placed throughout the touring area.

The museum played host to more than 100 special events, receptions, pre-game parties and Rupp Arena tours that included a visit to the Wildcat locker room. The museum closed its doors in July 2008 for lack of financial backing.

For the opening game in the new arena, the demand for tickets was so great that the University held a lottery for the general public after assigning seating for students, faculty and staff, and season ticket holders. Hundreds of applicants missed the cut and were placed on a "waiting list." More seats were added later on, increasing the capacity to more than 24,000 for basketball. A UK record 24,340 fans watched Kentucky beat Louisville, 89-66, on Dec. 23, 1995 in Rupp Arena.

Since the fall of 1976, the arena has served as home to four national championship teams. Three other Wildcat teams have advanced to the Final Four. Eight seasons have witnessed the Cats go unbeaten at home. They win ninety percent of their games in the arena.

Dominating the Lexington Center complex is Rupp Arena

Prior to 2004/05, Rupp Arena played host to 405 UK games, countless KHSAA Sweet 16's, a number of NBA exhibitions, 10 NCAA Tournaments, three SEC Tournaments and two Ohio Valley Conference Tournaments. With so many unforgettable moments, the old floor still maintained a value to hoop fans across the Bluegrass and beyond. Therefore, officials made pieces of the relic available for public sale, with proceeds going to the UK Basketball Museum, the Kentucky High School Athletic Association and to help offset the costs of the new playing floor. Thanks to an auction of additional sections, like coaching boxes and lettered end zones, the old floor generated more than $250,000.

Freedom Hall

Freedom Hall in Louisville is not considered a home floor for UK basketball, but neither is it a hostile environment. Since the Louisville facility opened in 1957 the Wildcats have won 75 percent of the games they played there. They established a then-Freedom Hall attendance record in1993 when 20,060 fans watched the Cats defeat Indiana, 81-78.

The Wildcats began playing in Louisville in 1908, when Louisville Coliseum defeated them, 30-18. They defeated the University of Louisville, 26-23, in 1914, lost to the Cards, 26-15, the following year, and beat them again, 32-24, in 1916. Two years later, UK lost to Centre College, 22-12, in a state championship game played in Louisville. The Wildcats defeated the Cards there in 1922 and did not play again in Louisville until the 1936/37 season, when Notre Dame beat them, 41-28.

Most of the early games were played in the old Jefferson County Armory. Kentucky's "Fiddlin' Five" christened the new

30

building by winning the 1958 NCAA title there with victories over Temple and Seattle. Kentucky teams have since played one or more games in the hall every season. Their overall record in the city of Louisville was 125-33. It was (60-18 in Freedom Hall) entering the 2011-12 season. UK held a 23-9 margin over Notre Dame in games played in Louisville.

Chapter Three
The Early Coaches

The lineage of coaching greats runs deep as the Kentucky hills. All Wildcat fans know about Adolph Rupp and his years of basketball success, but even before Rupp, the UK program enjoyed success. It was not without a little trial-and-error, however, as the first real coach of a Kentucky basketball team, Walter Mustaine, reluctantly fulfilled his coaching duties.

Walter W.H. Mustaine did not pose with the UK basketball team in 1904, but he was more than happy to surround himself with members of his fine gym squad. Indian clubs and tumbling were more important to the father of UK basketball than was the roundball.

Although the University of Kentucky listed Mustaine as the coach during basketball's first seven years at the school, he filled that position in name only. Student managers ran the team.

"None of us knew much about the game," Tommy Bryant recalled. "We knew what 'center-jump' was and that's about all. Mustaine had a wonderful team of tumblers and taught a class in swinging Indian clubs, but he didn't know or care much about basketball. He didn't want us basketball players getting in the way of his gym pets.

Dr. J. Conley Elliott, another member of the group that met with Mustaine, recalled 50 years later that the players purchased their own uniforms. He said the school hung iron hoops on the balcony at each end of the gym.

"Mustaine came to see us practice twice during the season," Dr. H. H. Downing said, "and he remained only a few minutes each time."

Wylie B. Wendt served as student manager of the 1906 State team. He recalled there was no such thing as a coach back then. "I was a one-man operation," he said in a 1974 interview. "I made the schedule, printed the tickets, collected the money, paid the bills, and took charge of the team on the road."

When the school decided to hire a basketball coach in 1910, the search committee focused its efforts on football coach E. R. Sweetland. A powerfully built, silent native of Dryden, N. Y., Sweetland was a graduate of both Cornell and Syracuse universities. He was a four-sport star at Cornell, where he was an All-America football tackle and a member of the row team that established a new world's record in the paired-oar shell. He arrived in Lexington after successful football coaching tenures at Hamilton University, Colgate, Syracuse, and the Ohio State University, where he also produced championship track and basketball teams.

Sweetland accepted an offer to coach the UK basketball team and later to be named the university's director of athletics. He was technically UK's first true basketball coach.

Sweetland became ill shortly after Thanksgiving and was hospitalized until late January. The Wildcats won their first two games under Professor R. E. Spahr, who served as an interim. Then they lost five in a row, including an 87-17 whipping by Central, which still stands as the worst loss ever suffered by a UK team. Sweetland returned in late January and a loss at Rose Poly extended UK's string to six straight setbacks.

The unpredictable Sweetland left State after the 1910 football season to coach the boat crew at the University of Wisconsin. The university hired H. J. Iddings, track and field coach at Miami of Ohio, as his replacement. After the 1911 team finished 5-6, Sweetland returned to Lexington and coached the Wildcats to their first undefeated basketball season. In what the school newspaper described as "one glorious march from start to finish", the UK boys never trailed as they swept a nine-game schedule that included two wins over Vanderbilt to inaugurate the series. It would be 42 years before a UK team would experience another undefeated season.

Sweetland is generally credited with bringing UK basketball from near extinction to a major sport at the school. After coaching the 1912 football team to a 7-2-0 record, he resigned abruptly due to an embarrassing incident where an on-campus act of arson occurred. Two former students and the athletic department were implicated in the event.

During the period between 1913 and 1928, twelve different men coached the UK basketball teams. The group included J. J. Tigert, 5-3 in 1913; Alpha Brumage, 18-7 in 1914-15; James Park, 8-6 in 1916; W. P. Tuttle, 4-6 in 1917; S. A. Boles, 9-2-1 in 1918; Andrew Gill, 6-8 in 1919; George Buchheit, 44-27 in 1920-24; C. O. Applegran, 13-8 in 1925; Ray Eklund, 15-3 in 1926; Basil Hayden, 3-13 in 1927; John Mauer, 40-14 in 1928-30, and Adolph Rupp, who soon gave up football duties.

The only non-football assistant in that long list of basketball coaches since Sweetland was Basil Hayden, UK's first All-American, and a member of the 1921 SIAA champions. When Ray Eklund unexpectedly resigned as basketball coach after a 15-3 record during the 1926 season, the university desperately asked Hayden to fill the post.

"I coached at Stanford High School and at Kentucky Wesleyan after leaving UK," Hayden said in 1974. "I had been in the insurance business when they asked me to coach until they could get somebody else. I knew it was going to be tough."

He started the season with a lineup of football players that the local press called "a comedy of errors". They displayed a remarkable ability to miss shots, walk with the ball, step on opponents' toes, and commit personal fouls. They had no incentive except when they played Centre, which had defeated them in football.

They defeated Centre twice and Florida once for a 3-13 record, which would stand as the school's last losing season until a probation-ridden UK team finished 13-19 in 1982/83. Kentucky compiled an overall record of 163-134-1 from 1903 to 1927.

Mustaine and others (1903-1909)
Kentucky Record (21-35)

Edwin W. Sweetland

Edwin W. Sweetland (1910, 1912)
Kentucky Record (13-8)
1909–1910 4-8
1911-1912 9-0

Prof. R. E. Spahr substituted for Sweetland when Sweetland was hospitalized early in the 1910 season. Central beat the Wildcats, 87-17, their worst defeat ever.

Sweetland also coached the 1910
(7-2) and 1912 (7-2) UK football teams

Harold J. Iddings

Harold J. Iddings (1911)
Kentucky Record 5-6)

The Lexington Leader referred to UK's 5-6 record as
"remarkable", considering the late start of practice and the use of
ILL instead of AAU rules on a northern trip that cost them
consecutive losses to Ohio Wesleyan, Otterbein and Christ
Church of Cincinnati.

J. J. Tigert

J. J. Tigert (1913)
Kentucky Record (5-3)

Tigert was a philosophy professor who served two years as coach of the UK Ladies basketball team; He also coached Wildcat football teams in 1915 (6-1-1) and 1916 (4-1-2).

Tigert later served as U. S. Commissioner of Education, and as president of the University of Florida.

Alpha Brumage

Alpha Brumage (1914, 1915)
Kentucky (Record (18-7)

1913-14 11-2
1914-1915 (7-5)
When Sweetland took a leave of absence, Brumage
coached both the UK basketball and football teams (11-5).

James Park

James Park (1916)
Kentucky Record (8-6)

Park was captain of the 1913 UK football team.
He earned a basketball letter on the 1914 Wildcat team
(12-2) that christened the new Woodland Avenue Auditorium on
East High Street with a 59-12 win over Louisville YMHA.

W. P. Tuttle

W. P. Tuttle (1917)
Kentucky Record (4-6)

Tuttle won four letters each in basketball and football at UK. He set a UK football record by scoring 40 points (6 TD, 7 PAT) in an 80-0 win over Maryville in 1914.

Tuttle later ran a pineapple plantation in Hawaii.

S. A. "Daddy" Boles

S A. "Daddy" Boles (1918)
Kentucky Record (9-2-1)*

Boles served in various capacities at the University, the longest, from 1917 through 1933, as athletic director. In this post he helped bring Basketball Coach Adolph Rupp to UK in 1930.

He was UK's head football coach for a year and in 1918 he was head basketball coach. He also served as assistant football coach for several years while he was athletic director.

After leaving the post of athletic director, Boles was made professor of physical education and business manager of athletics, holding the latter post from 1934 through 1936.

Following this he was ticket sales manager for the Athletics Department until 1946. Boles also was golf coach from 1938 through 1946.

He then served as a manger of the veterans' housing project until 1955 when he went on change of work status, being assigned as historian of the projects.

The unique tie game between UK and Kentucky Wesleyan resulted from a scorer's error discovered after the game.

Andrew Gill (1919)
Kentucky Record) (6-8)

A flu epidemic caused authorities to close the school three months at the beginning of the school year and not resume its work until the middle of January. They dropped a two-point decision to Georgetown, their first loss to the Tigers since 1910.

George Buchheit

George Buchheit (1920-1924)
Kentucky Record (44-27)

1919-1920-11-13 When the university hired Fred J. Murphy as football coach in 1924, they asked Buchheit to remain as basketball coach. He chose to move to Trinity College (now Duke University) in Durham, N.C.

1920-1921-13-1
1921-1922 10-6
922-1923-3-10
1923-1924 13-3

C. O. Applegran (1925)
Kentucky Record (13-8)

Applegran was a former University of Illinois star whose Wildcat team played their first game in the new Alumni Gym. They defeated Cincinnati.28-23.

Ray Eklund (1926)
Kentucky Record (15-3)

Eklund drilled his team along the same lines as had Applegran and Buchheit. He rewarded them with two sets of uniforms, a first for a UK basketball team. One set consisted of white, woolen jerseys with "Kentucky" spelled across the chest while the breeches were solid blue with a white border. The other set had solid blue jerseys and breeches with white border and white letters.

Basil Hayden

Basil Hayden (1927)
Kentucky Record (3-13)

UK's first basketball All-American suffered from tonsillitis at his first game as coach of the Wildcats. He directed the team with penciled messages to team captain Paul Jenkins. . Cincinnati beat them, 48-10. It was UK's worst defeat since losing to Wabash, by 46 points in 1925.

Johnny Mauer

Johnny Mauer (1928-30)
Kentucky Record (40-14)

1927-28	12	6
1928-29	12	5
1929-30	16	3
Total	40	14

John Mauer played in the Illinois backfield with Red Grange, his roommate, and was an All-Conference forward in basketball. He brought to UK an upgraded version of the "Illinois system," which the school newspaper described as an "impenetrable man-to-man defense," and an offense where everyone was able to shoot, pass and dribble. Mauer introduced to the South a slow-breaking attack built around a complicated short-pass game, which utilized hitherto unknown outside screening plays.

The Wildcats won forty and lost fourteen of the games they played during Mauer's three years at the university. They finished the 1930 season with a 16-3 record. Returning home after losing to Duke in the championship game of the Southeastern Conference Tournament, a mob of boosters shoulder-carried them through the railroad terminal and marched down Main Street.

The school newspaper described Mauer as the "Moses" of Kentucky basketball, a prophet who had led the game out of its slam-bang, hit-and-miss style of former years and developed it along the lines of the machine-like precision of football. He had changed the Wildcats from doormat to drawing card and his influence had become felt throughout the South. Mauer seemed destined to go down in Southern basketball annals as the pioneer of a new system, the father, so to speak, of Dixie basketball.

Less than two months later, the Athletic Council gave Mauer a token raise, while giving more generously to the football staff, which had compiled a 6-1-1 season. Mauer resigned in a huff, much to the chagrin of the council, and accepted the head-coaching job at Miami University in Ohio.

Chapter Four
Rupp Era

Adolph Rupp

Rupp wanted to be a banker, but circumstances deemed otherwise. Times were hard when he graduated from the University of Kansas in 1923, and banking jobs were few and far between. Besides, he was born to coach.

Adolph was six years old when Halstead High School won the first of two consecutive state championships. "I've never forgotten the enthusiasm that spread throughout our district," he said 50 years later. "Don't tell me winning isn't important."

The Halstead basketball program hit rock bottom by the time Adolph enrolled as a freshman in 1915. Jeptha Carl Stone replaced W. A. Lee as the basketball coach and admittedly knew little about the game. Adolph played sparingly during his sophomore year, but Stone said the young farm boy seemed interested in what few plays they ran. The weekly newspaper began publishing the game scores during Rupp's junior year. He averaged 19 points a game, which was huge in those days.

The players elected Adolph as their team captain his senior year. Stone entered the military and the new coach knew so little about the game that Adolph took over the operation. He scored a career high 33 points in a 60-30 win over Burrton and averaged 19.1 points a game. Halstead lost to Nickerson in the district tournament.

Adolph worked a variety of odd jobs, both indoors and in the fields, to pay his high school expenses. He saved some money and earned enough extra in the summer to enroll in the University of Kansas.

"I had my sights set on going into banking, and the coaching of basketball was the furthest thing from my mind," Rupp said. "But things were pretty hard, and I returned to the university to work on an advance degree after walking the streets of Topeka and Wichita."

The university placed Rupp in a teaching job at Burr Oak, Kansas, which also entailed coaching the basketball and football teams. When the football players showed up in overalls, Rupp and the school principal finally rounded up some uniforms. Rupp said they were substandard and he ended up paying for them. They played basketball in an old barn renovated for a skating rink.

Member of the 1930 UK football coaching staff are Len Miller, Adolph Rupp, Birkett Pribble, Elmer Gilb, Harry Gamage, Bernie Shively, and Pete Drury.

Rupp played on two national championship basketball teams coached by the great Phog Allen at Kansas. Dr. James A. Naismith, who invented basketball at the Springfield, Mass., YMCA in 1896, was the university's director of physical education. He gave the physical examinations to incoming freshmen. Rupp attended Naismith's classes in hygiene and became acquainted with him at basketball practice sessions, which Naismith often attended.

As a member of Allen's "Meatpackers", Rupp entered a game after the outcome was evident. While riding the bench, he absorbed what transpired there and on the floor, never dreaming he would later put that knowledge to use.

Rupp coached at the high school level for five years. His path to greatness started when Kentucky was looking to hire a replacement for John Mauer.

The Athletic Council received seventy applicants for the vacant position. They narrowed the list to a man from Indiana and Adolph F. Rupp, an unknown high school coach whose Freeport, Illinois teams had compiled a 59-21 record during his four years there. They had finished second two times and were champions twice in their district, won a sectional and finished third in the state.

Two university officials went to the Lexington railway to greet a 6-foot-2, slightly portly young man who dressed conservatively, combed his hair neatly, spit-shined his shoes, and carried himself well. He looked like a preacher.

The route through Lexington went through a slum area known as Pralltown. Arriving late for lunch, the trio settled for cold fish, cornbread, and coffee. "I thought the people of Kentucky had poor houses," Rupp said, "and they didn't eat so good".

Rupp said his high school teams at Freeport played in a much better facility than Alumni Gym, which Rupp called a "little peanut-huller," and although they offered him exactly the same salary he was making in high school, he decided not to pass up an opportunity to coach at a major university.

Pat Harmon, a Freeport native and the sports editor of the Cincinnati Post and Times-Star, asked a council member why they hired Rupp.

"Because he told us he was the best damned basketball coach in the United States," the administrator replied", and he convinced us that he was."

To his players, fans, family, and the media Adolph Rupp was many things, some good, some bad, few neutral, but no one expressed doubts about his coaching ability. A heavy-set man, and a pleasant one when he wasn't coaching, Rupp was dynamic, controversial and colorful. He became known early on as the "Basketball Baron of the Bluegrass" because of the success of his teams and the Hereford cattle that he bred on his two tobacco-based farms outside of Lexington. The honorary title suggested an arrogance that Rupp often displayed, both on and off the court.

Since his favorite coaching attire out of superstition, was usually a double-breasted brown suit, he also picked up the nickname of the "Man in the Brown Suit". At other times he was referred to as "Mr. Basketball". Rupp took his Wildcat teams into tiny, old gymnasiums, new field houses, Madison Square

Garden, and other big-city arenas, where he was often hooted and despised, but always respected.

Michael Bradley, of The Sporting News, depicted Rupp as a complex person who was sarcastic and demanding of his players. "He was hardheaded and too proud," Bradley said, "but he was a giant on the basketball court, and his accomplishments made Kentucky Basketball what it is today".

The Southern media labeled him "Old Rupp and Ready" because of his bench antics, which included profanity and vicious verbal attacks on persons on and off the floor. He became known as the "Most Hated Man in Dixie", mostly because his teams consistently beat everybody in the South, and he rubbed it in. "The boys didn't do what I told them to do", was a favorite Rupp expression. "Guess I'll have to take them to the woodshed."

Rupp had 876 wins when he retired in 1972, a mark that stood until North Carolina's Dean Smith, also a former Kansas player, moved three ahead during the 1997 season.

"Adolph was absolutely impervious to criticism," Rupp's longtime assistant Harry Lancaster said, "thinking that anyone who dared criticize him must be a complete fool".

Lancaster said Rupp's image—arrogant, egocentric and sometimes just plain rude—came from a relentless dedication to success. "Nobody is a really good loser, but that is an easy way out. Rupp wouldn't pretend to take losses easily. He was a perfectly honest man."

Bear Bryant, whose football office was down the hall from Rupp's in Alumni Gym, said you either hated Rupp or you didn't like him. "There was no middle ground," Bryant said. "He had that abrasive way of talking and dealing with people, and if you didn't like it you didn't like him."

Rhythm through repetition was a key to his precision-drilled teams. Rupp was such a stickler for details that players ran a play over and over until they got it right. He organized practice sessions down to the precise minute.

Rupp considered himself a professor, courtesy of a Teacher's Certificate earned at Columbia University during summer vacations at Freeport. He taught a course in "advanced basketball", which some considered a likely refuge from the arts and sciences. Rupp insisted that the course was invaluable for athletes who intended to become coaches.

Moreover, he proclaimed himself the best professor at the university because all his students got A's. "What kind of professor gives failing grades?" he asked. "It just proves he didn't teach his students anything."

Rupp possessed a drawl that begged imitation and made his stories most entertaining. In constant demand as a speaker, he could draw from a wealth of material, Bible School and from his love of poetry. He was a psychologist who knew which player to treat cautiously and whom to scold; his biting sarcasm sometimes had a player on the edge of tears. The feeling existed that if you couldn't stand the heat, get out of the arena. Kentucky's all-time leading scorer Dan Issel was intimidated by Rupp; however, he differed in his view of the Baron.

"There are players who need a kick in the seat to be motivated, and there are players who need a pat on the back to be motivated," Dan Issel told Jamie Vaught. "Coach Rupp's philosophy was to kick everybody in the seat of the pants and if they weren't strong enough to take it, he didn't want you on his basketball team."

Unlike his mentor, the legendary Kansas coach Phog Allen, who took a personal interest in his players, Rupp kept his boys at a distance. "If I wanted to be a daddy to them," he said, "I would take them out on the farm and put them to work."

The other side of Rupp projected the image of a dedicated family man who lived with his wife Esther and son Herky in a modest home a few blocks from the university. He cared little about what newspapers outside the community wrote about him, but he didn't want his family reading bad things about him in the local press.

Rupp was a good story source, always ready to provide a quotable quote. He welcomed reporters to his hotel room on the road, often plying them with food and drink. While his football counterparts at UK kept their phone numbers unlisted, Rupp's was an open book. "I didn't get where I am by NOT talking to the press," he said.

The Baron had a close-knit circle of friends that included bankers and other local businessmen whom he assigned such courtside tasks as keeping the scorebook and time clock.

Although gregarious in public, Rupp was calm and placid at home, catering to Esther's every wish. He professed a lifetime fear of women; he never strayed from the fold.

Adolph Rupp (1931-1972),
Kentucky Record (876-180)

UK football coach Harry Gamage assigned Rupp to assist freshman coach Brinkley Barnett. Rupp also kept statistics during the home games.

"I had a good relationship with all the UK coaches except Chet Wynne," Rupp said. "He told me the campus wasn't big enough for both of us. I told him to start packing because I wasn't going anywhere."

Season	W	L	
1930-31	15	3	
1931-32	15	2	
1932-33	21	3	
1933-34	16	1	
1934-35	19	2	
1935-36	15	6	
1936-37	17	5	
1937-38	13	5	
1938-39	16	4	
1939-40	15	6	
1940-41	17	8	
1941-42	19	6	(NCAA)

1942-43	17	6	
1943-44	19	2	
1944-45	22	4	(NCAA)
1945-46	28	2	(NIT-1)
1946-47	34	3	(NIT-2)
1947-48	36	3 (NCAA-1)	
1948-49	32	2	(NCAA-1)
1949-50	25	5	
1950-51	32	2	(NCAA-1)
1951-52	29	3	(NCAA)
1952-53		No Team	
1953-54	25	0	(Undefeated)
1954-55	23	3	(NCAA)
1955-56	20	6	(NCAA)
1956-57	23	5	NCAA)
1957-58	20	6	(NCAA-1)
1958-59	24	3	(NCAA)
1959-60	18	7	
1960-61	19	9	(NCAA)
1961-62	23	3	(NCAA)
1962-63	16	0	
1963-64	21	6	(NCAA)
1964-65	15	10	
1965-66	27	2	(NCAA)
1966-67	13	13	
1967-68	22	5	(NCAA)
1968-69	23	5	(NCAA)
1969-70	26	2	(NCAA)
1970-71	22	6	(NCAA)
1971-72	21	7	(NCAA)

College basketball has seen few coaches who have been more dominant than Adolph Rupp. In winning 876 games in 41 years of coaching, Rupp set a remarkable standard of excellence for others to follow. Rupp was a master of developing local talent. In his early years at UK, he took more than 80 percent of his players from Kentucky and turned them into champions.

Rupp possessed an intense desire to win and instilled that feeling in his players. He promoted a sticky man-to-man defense, and a relentless fast break offense that battered opponents into defeat. His UK teams won four NCAA titles (1948, '49, '51, and '58), one Olympic Gold Medal (1948), one NIT Championship (1946), 27 Southeastern Conference titles, and five Sugar Bowl championships. They were 397-75 (84.1%) against SEC competition. In the conference tournament, Rupp's Wildcats were 57-6, winning 13 titles in 19 appearances.

Adolph Rupp and assistant coach Paul McBrayer made the Wildcats national contenders in the early 1940s

U.S. Olympic Basketball Team—Front row, L to R Ralph Beard, Kenny Rollins, Cliff Barker, Dale Barnstable Back Row Joe Holland, Alex Groza, Coach Adolph Rupp, Wallace Jones, Jim Line

Before the 1948 Olympic Trials, the U.S. Basketball Committee chose a 14-member Olympic squad that consisted of five members each from each team in the championship bracket and four from the other teams in each bracket. The coach of the winning team would be the head coach, with the coach of the second place team serving as associate coach.

The squad members were UK's Barker, Beard, Groza, Jones and Rollins; Phillips 66's Bob Kurland, Jesse Remick, Gordon Carpenter, R. C. Pitts, and Lew Beck: Vince Boryla of the Denver Nuggets; Don Barksdale of the Oakland Bittners; Jack Robinson of Baylor; and Ray Lumpp of NYU.

The U.S. defeated Switzerland, 86-21; Czechoslovakia, 53-28; Argentina, 59-57; and Peru, 61-33, to place in the final elimination. They trailed Argentina by halftime, but bounced

56

back to win by two points. They easily dispatched Egypt, Peru, Uruguay, Mexico, and France for the championship.

Rupp said it was the biggest thrill of his life to see five of his boys stand on the podium while the National Anthem was being played and get medals as world champions.

Rupp was voted SEC Coach of the Year honors on seven occasions and received the honor nationally four times. In 1967, the Columbus (Ohio) Touchdown Club named him its Coach of the Century. Two years later, he was inducted into the Basketball Hall of Fame.

Rupp was by far the most prominent of the 20 coaches who guided UK basketball to 1,888 victories and only 572 losses from 1903 to 2005. Both the total of wins and the winning percentage of 82.2% are all-time national records. However, the other 19 coaches are much a part of the winning tradition. But the modern era begins with Rupp.

Joe B. and Adolph

Rupp demanded 100 percent from his players at all times, pushing them to great levels of success. Twenty-four players earned All-American honors, seven captured Olympic gold medals, and 28 played professionally. A four-time Coach of the Year, Rupp established a winning tradition at Kentucky rivaled only by John Wooden at UCLA. Rupp Arena stands as a monument for the coach who made Kentucky basketball synonymous with greatness.

Chapter Five
Post Rupp

Joe B. Hall won 297 games, an NIT title and an NCAA title

Joe B. Hall (1973-1985)

Hall was born and raised on a farm 20 minutes north of the university, where practically everyone bled Kentucky-blue. As kids, he and his older brother Bill would listen to Kentucky basketball broadcasts. They would set up coffee cans in bed and throw paper balls into them. They would play the game right along with the radio. Hall still has some of the stats they compiled while listening to those games.

He lettered three years each in basketball and football at Cynthiana High School. He also captained both teams. Eastern Kentucky State Teachers College invited him to Richmond for a second tryout in football, but Hall opted to play basketball at UK.

That was during the "Fabulous Five" era, when the UK talent pool was so deep that four All-Americans sat on the bench. "I was the only kid on the squad," Hall said. "Everybody else was coming out of the service. I was the only guy who didn't shave." He also was the only player to wear glasses, which he taped to his temples.

Hall played one year of junior varsity ball. He was the only player brought up the following year from the freshman group. "We chose Joe over players that were bigger, stronger, and faster, but he had a feel for the game that is hard to coach," Rupp said in 1975. "We had so many experienced players ahead of him that he asked for a transfer." Rupp called his friend Lon Varnell at the University of the South at Sewanee, who was glad to get a player of Hall's caliber. Joe B. set a school scoring record his first year at Sewanee.

Following his college career, Hall toured Europe with the Harlan Globetrotters in 1951. After failing a tryout with the Chicago Stags, he returned home and became a salesman for the Heinz Company. He also completed requirements for a Master's Degree at UK.

Hall began his coaching career at Shepherdsville (Ky.) High School in 1956. During two seasons there, he won a Conference Coach of the Year selection. He spent the next five years (57-50 record) at Regis College in Denver, where he defeated Oklahoma State, St. Louis and some other ranked teams. When Regis deemphasized athletics, Hall coached one season at Central Missouri (19-6). They won their conference championship and competed in the 1975 NCAA Tournament.

Kentucky Gov. Wendell Ford and Joe B.

       Hall attended a basketball clinic in St. Louis that featured Rupp as the guest lecturer. During the course of his presentation Rupp pointed Hall out and recognized him as one of his former players and a promising young coach. He later invited Joe B. to his room and asked him to return to Kentucky. Hall returned to UK as an assistant to Rupp on July 1, 1965.

       Rupp primarily wanted a recruiter, but Hall insisted on a share of the coaching. When he saw the poor recruiting setup at UK, he reorganized the entire system and hit the recruiting trail. Hall estimated that he traveled 25,000 miles to watch 175 games and scout 2,500 players annually during those early years.

       Hall's recruiting paid big dividends for UK. The 1965/1966 varsity compiled a 13-13 record, the worst in Rupp's career, but a freshman team, recruited mostly by Hall, won 18 of 20 games played. It featured such future outstanding stars as Dan Issel, Mike Casey, and Mike Pratt.

       Joe B. was the logical successor to Rupp, but he grew tired of waiting for the reluctant baron to retire and accepted the job as head coach at St. Louis University in April 1969. He returned only after UK administrators, including Rupp, assured him he would become the next head coach.

Before taking over the program in 1972/73, Hall recruited a freshmen class that included four Mr. Basketball's—Kentucky (Jimmy Dan Conner), Illinois (Bob Guyette), Indiana (Mike Flynn), and Ohio (Kevin Grevey). He coached the team to an undefeated freshman season. \Meanwhile Rupp and his assistants, Dick Parsons and Gale Catlett, guided the varsity to a 21-7 record that ended with a loss to Florida State in the Mideast Regional.

One funny story about Coach Hall occurred just before tip-off of UK's semifinal game against Syracuse in the 1975 Final Four, the Wildcats were a tight bunch, sitting in the locker room and wondering what wisdom the coaches would impart.

Hall entered the room and spotted a large trash can with a plastic liner across the room. He walked over, climbed into the container, and pulled the plastic over his head.

After a few seconds, which seemed much longer, Hall climbed out of the barrel and said, "Let's go play some basketball". Kentucky beat the Orangemen, 95-79.

Coach Hall compiled an overall record of 297 wins and 100 losses during his 13 years as head coach at UK. His teams made three Final Four appearances, winning the NCAA championship in 1978. They won eight SEC titles and one SEC Tournament in six tries.

While Coach Rupp saw 37 of his players drafted by the NBA, Hall had 23 players drafted during his 13-year tenure, five in the first round. He earned National Coach of the Year honors in 1978 and SEC Coach of the Year awards on four different occasions. He had seven players win All-America honors 11 times and nine All-SEC selections on 11 occasions.

Hall retired from coaching in 1984, keeping a vow made when he first entered the profession. He became a member of the Naismith Basketball Hall of Fame in 2013

UK Record: 297-100 (74.8, overall record—373—156 (72.5), 19 years
1972-73 20 8

1973-74
1974-75 26 5 (NCAA)
1975-76 20 10 (NIT-1)

1976-77 26 4 (NCAA)
1977-78 30 2 (NCAA-1)
1978-79 19 12 (NIT)
1979-80 20 6 (NCAA)
1980-81 22 6 (NCAA)
1981- 82 22 8 (NCAA)
1982-83 23 8 (NCAA)
1983-84 29 5 (NCAA)
1984-85 18 13 (NCAA)
Total 297 100

Eddie Sutton

Eddie Sutton
UK Record: 88 – 39

Years Coached: 1985-86 to 1988-89 (4 seasons)
Date of Birth: March 12, 1936
Hometown: Bucklin, KS

Alma Mater: Oklahoma A&M [1958]

Record at Kentucky

1985-86 32 4 (NCAA)
1986-87 13 11
1987-88 27 6
1988-89 13 19
Total 85 40

Sutton came to UK in 1985 from the University of Arkansas, where his Razorback teams appeared in nine consecutive NCAA tournaments. The school had made only four previous appearances to the tournament. Arkansas gave UK a tremendous battle before losing to the Wildcats in the 1978 Final Four.

The university was playing host to the 1985 Final Four when a search committee sought a replacement for Joe B. Hall. When UK athletic director Cliff Hagan notified Sutton, the job was his, Sutton replied, "I didn't think you'd ever call. Believe me, I would have crawled all the way to Lexington".

Like Rupp and North Carolina's Dean Smith, Sutton was a native of Kansas. He played guard on Hank Iba's 1958 Oklahoma State team that advanced to the Elite Eight of the NCAA Tournament. Sutton began his coaching career as a graduate assistant to Iba He advanced through the high school and junior college ranks. Sutton took over the Creighton program in the fall of 1969. He spent five seasons in Omaha; his teams were 82-50 over a five-year period.

During 11 seasons at Arkansas, Sutton's Razorbacks amassed a record of 260-75, an average of 23.6 victories a season. He was twice named national Coach of the Year, in 1977 and 1978. Sutton earned four titles as top coach in the Southwestern Conference.

While controversy cast a shadow over the UK program, Sutton's first Wildcat team (1985-86) posted a 32-4 record and finished first in the SEC with 17 wins and one loss. They defeated both Alabama and LSU three times that season, and faced them again in the NCAA regional. They defeated Alabama again, but lost to LSU, 59-57, in the Southeast semifinals.

Although the signing of Rex Chapman and Derrick Miller helped fill the gap left by Kenny Walker, Wildcat hopes suffered a crippling blow when Winston Bennett, their best inside player, underwent surgery for a pre-season knee injury. They managed an 18-11 season, mediocre by UK standards, losing to Auburn, 79-72, in the SEC tournament finale and to Ohio State, 91-77 in the regional.

The Wildcats won their first 10 games played the following year. They lost five SEC games, but won the regular season and tournament titles. They won two NCAA games, but lost to Villanova in the regional.

With UK investigators at the door and players leaving en masse, Kentucky staggered to a 13-19 record in 1988/89. It was the school's first losing season since 1927. The NCAA put the UK on probation for three years because of recruiting and academic violations. The sanctions decreased scholarships, limited television exposure and forced the Cats to surrender their 1988 SEC titles and NCAA victories. Sutton and his staff left in the aftermath, as did UK athletics director Cliff Hagan.

Rick Pitino

Rick Pitino (1990-1997)
b. Sept. 18, 1952, New York, N. Y.

UK Record: 219-50 (81.4%)

1989-90 14-14
1990-91   22- 6
1991-92   29- 7 (NCAA Final 8)
1992-93   30- 4 (NCAA Final Four)
1993-94   27- 7 (NCAA) (Undefeated)
1994-95   28- 5 (NCAA Final 8)
1995-96   34- 2 (NCAA Champion)
1996-97   35- 5 (NCAA Final Four)

When Kentucky began a search for a basketball coach to replace Eddie Sutton, Robert Lindsay, a local disc jockey at WVLK-Radio, announced the first week of May that he would camp on a billboard until a new coach was named. Lindsay set up housekeeping 20 feet above the highway the first week of May. Ralph Hacker's staff at the station supplied Lindsay with a tent and a recliner. They even wired his TV for cable.

Pitino visited the campus just before Memorial Day. He accepted the job in early June. On his first day as coach, he stopped by to notify Lindsay that he could down from the billboard.

Rick Pitino arrived in Kentucky dressed in an Armani suit and Gucci shoes and carrying a suitcase full of impressive credentials. The cultural shock rocked a fan base that consisted of many persons who had grown up wearing blue denim shirts and bib overalls. However, practically everyone who was anybody in UK basketball knew about the city slicker who had rebuilt Boston U., Providence, and the New York Knicks.

Two years earlier, many Wildcat fans sat in Louisville's Freedom Hall or watched on television as Pitino's Providence Friars defeated a fine Alabama team en route to the 1987 NCAA Final Four. They wondered how C. M. Newton had convinced Rick to leave the Big Apple, where he had rejuvenated the Knicks. Surely he must have read the Sports Illustrated article, Kentucky's Shame? Did he really think he could repeat the rebuilding programs at Boston College, Providence, and New York?

"What C. M. did was take his time, find the coach he wanted, then go after him with every ounce of energy he had available," Dick Weiss wrote. "And the man C.M. came up with in what has proved to be a stroke of genius was a fiery, aggressive New York Italian-American who was as different from most Kentuckians as night is from day."

Wildcat fans "took to" Pitino, as people say in the hills. They loved his up-tempo style, three-point shooting, and pressing defenses. He said Kentucky would win again, and they believed him. Most experts ceded him eight wins at most when he opened the 1989/90 campaign with the remnants of the previous year.

Eddie Sutton had recruited a lineup of Rex Chapman, Eric Manuel, and Sean Sutton at guard, Chris Mills and Shawn Kemp at forward, LeRon Ellis at center, and a bench that consisted of Deron Feldhaus, Richie Farmer, Reggie Hanson,

John Pelphrey, and Sean Woods. It was a Final Four lineup waiting to happen.

Most of the marquee names were gone by the time Pitino arrived. Chapman turned pro after his sophomore year. Ellis was UK's best shot-blocker and second-leading rebounder. He transferred to Syracuse. Sean Sutton spent a year a t Lexington Community College and eventually joined his father at Oklahoma State. Jeff Brassow, Derrick Miller, and Jonathan Davis rounded out the squad.

PITINO INTRODUCES THE 3'S

Pitino introduced the players and the fans to the "3's" and they loved it. The Wildcats put up 53 treys during an opening 116-113 overtime loss to Southwest Louisiana. They made 21 threes during a 121-110 loss to North Carolina. "Pitino's Bombinos" set six national records that year. They shot an NCAA record 810 three's, making 281. Derrick Miller made 99 of 289. He made eight three's in games against Kansas, North Carolina, and Tennessee.

Every time the Cats made a three, the students section celebrated by taping a blue and white "3" card to the Rupp Arena wall near the scoreboard, starting a new tradition.

Pitino worked one of his miracles that first year at UK. He took the remnants of a scandal-ridden program and compiled a 14-14 record; by past UK standards, that would be a tragedy, but the fans were ecstatic. The members of those first two staffs that Pitino assembled formed an impressive group of future head coaches. Tubby Smith served alongside Ralph Willard of Holy Cross, North Carolina State's Herb Sendek, and Florida's Billy Donovan, and Bernadette Mattox, former coach of the UK women's team.

During his eight years at Kentucky, Pitino coached three All-Americans, Jamal Mashburn, Tony Delk and Ron Mercer, and eight players who were drafted by the NBA, including six in the first round (three lottery picks). Kentucky's All-SEC selections included Reggie Hanson ('90, '91), Derrick Miller ('90), John Pelphrey ('91), Jamal Mashburn ('91, '92, '93), Travis Ford ('93), Tony Delk ('95, '96), Antoine Walker ('96).

Pitino guided the Wildcats to three NCAA Final Four appearances in his last five years at Kentucky, winning the 1996 NCAA Championship and reaching the national title game in 1997. In eight seasons his Wildcats, compiled a 219-50 record while winning two league crowns and posting an impressive 17-1 record in the Southeastern Conference Tournament.

Orlando "Tubby Smith"

Orlando "Tubby Smith" (1998-2004)
b. June 30, 1951, Scotland, Md.

UK Record: 191-52

Kentucky Totals
1997-98   35-4 (NCAA Champ)
1998-99   28-9 (NCAA 8)
1999-00   23-10 (NCAA 32)
2000-01   24-10 (NCAA 16)

2001-02	22-10 (NCAA 16)
2002-03	32-4 (NCAA 8)
2003-04	27-5 (NCAA 32)

Total (7 years) 191-52 (78.6%)

If Kentuckians had any doubts about Tubby Smith, they were quickly dispelled during his first year as head coach of the Wildcats, when he won what all coaches and UK fans want- a national championship.

In the 1998 off-season, Tubby Smith picked up the Parent of the Year Award by Parent Magazine, the Victor Award by the Black Coaches Association and was even voted the "Sexiest Male Public Figure" in a reader's vote in a local magazine. The honors culminated when he was named the Kentucky Sportsman of the Year for 1998 in a statewide media vote, edging out the highly popular Tim Couch of the Kentucky football team.

"I had 16 brothers and sisters, and Saturday night was the only time we got to take a bath," Smith said. "When I got into that tub, I didn't want to get out."

Smith developed a group of experienced seniors and talented newcomers into a 35-4 team that gave Kentucky its second national championship in three years and seventh overall. Smith had become the first coach since Cincinnati's Ed Jucker in 1961 to win the national title in his first year at a school.

He was named National Coach of the Year by Basketball Weekly and Co-SEC Coach of the Year by The Associated Press. The New York Athletic Club presented him with the prestigious Winged Foot Award given to the coach of the national champions after each season.

Smith came to Kentucky in 1989 as a member of Rick Pitino's first UK staff. His first head coaching job came two years late at the University of Tulsa. He led the Golden Hurricanes (79-43) to the Missouri Valley Conference title in 1994 and 1995 as well as to the NCAA Tournament those years. He was twice named MVC coach of the year. Smith next coached Georgia to a 45-19 record, including a Sweet Sixteen berth. When UK needed a new coach after the 1996/97 season, Smith was the only person interviewed for the job.

During his first seven seasons (1997/98-2003/04) at UK, Smith led the Wildcats to one national championship, four SEC crowns, and five SEC Tournament titles, with five Sweet 16 finishes. In 2001, he totaled 100 wins quicker than any other Wildcat coach except Adolph Rupp, reaching the plateau in 130 games.

Over his 13 seasons as a head coach, Smith amassed 11 consecutive 20-win seasons. In 2004, he joined an elite group when he became the sixth head coach to win 300 games in 13 seasons or less, joining the likes of Roy Williams, Jim Boeheim and Nolan Richardson. Smith's career record was 315-114, and his 73.4 winning percentage sixth among active coaches entering the 2004/05 season. .

In NCAA Tournament play, Smith is tied for the sixth-best winning percentage among active coaches, trailing Duke's Mike Kryzewski and Michigan State's Tom Izzo, among others, with a sterling 24-10 record.

UK's triumphs in the 1998-99 season included six wins over teams ranked in the top 11. They defeated No. 2 Maryland and No. 4 Auburn, and recorded 13 wins over teams in the NCAA Tournament. When March arrived, Smith's squad won its seventh SEC Tournament title in eight years. The third-seeded Wildcats then competed in their eighth consecutive NCAA Tournament. They defeated Kansas, 92-88, in overtime, perhaps the most exciting game of the tourney. UK finished with a 28-9 record after losing to Michigan State in a regional final.

Since that time, Smith's Wildcats captured SCC championships in 2000, 2001, 2002, 2003, 2004, 2005. In 2002 they battled an amount of injuries and suspensions before being eliminated by Maryland, the eventual national champion, in the East Region Semifinals.

In 2003, a year in which Tubby Smith's coaching ranked among the very best in the 100 years of Kentucky basketball, the accolades arrived in a landslide. Smith snared all seven of the national honors recognized by the NCAA - AP, USBWA, Naismith, Basketball Times, The Sporting News, NABC, and CBS/Chevrolet. He became the first coach to sweep the list since Indiana's Bobby Knight captured all five in 1975. For good measure, Smith added honors from ESPN, Foxsports.com, the Black Coaches Association, and College Sports Television.

Kentucky established the nation's longest win streak in seven years, highlighted by a sweep of the SEC regular-season slate and tournament play (19-0), a feat that had not been accomplished in the league since 1952. His Wildcats finished No. 1 in the final Associated Press poll and Smith swept SEC and National Coach of the Year honors. Kentucky ended the season in the Elite Eight with a 32-4 record, becoming just the 11th team in school history to top the 30-win mark.

His 2004 Wildcat edition posted a 27-5 record, a sixth SEC Eastern Division title, another SEC Tournament championship and the school's ninth No. 1 seed in the NCAA Tournament while spending nearly the entire season ranked among the Nation's elite

Even today, comparisons exist between all of the coaches. But, isn't that part of being a loyal fan? Jeff Sheppard, in his book, Heart of a Champion, writes about the differences between Tubby Smith and Rick Pitino.

"Both men carry a tremendous intensity inside them, yet even with that, they bring it in a different way. Coach Pitino would yell at you to get back in line; Coach Smith can also yell, but it's those eyes, that look that lets you know you'd better straighten up."

"Coach Pitino motivated you by yelling at you. There was something about the way he did it that made us want to do anything for him. With Coach Smith, though, certain things are expected of you and if you fail to do them, then you're disappointing him."

Billy Clyde Gillispie

Billy Clyde Gillispie (2008-09)

Kentucky Record: 40-27

2008—18-13 (NCAA First Round)
2009—22-14 (NIT)

At 12:45 p. m on April 6, 2007, UK athletic director Mitch Barnhart announced Billy Gillispie as the new head coach of the Wildcats. Gillispie signed a memo that outlined his salary and benefits. The memo also stated that contract negotiations would be concluded with "every reasonable effort" within 60 days. Gillispie and the University never signed a formal contract.

In his first few months as UK coach, Gillispie signed high profile recruits Patrick Patterson and Alex Legion. Legion transferred six games into his first season at Kentucky. Gillispie's first season got off to a rocky start, being routed 68-84 by unranked Gardner–Webb in Rupp Arena in the second game of the season. This loss dropped the Wildcats from the AP Top 25 poll, where they did not return for the remainder of the season. The Wildcats improved their record during conference play, achieving a 12–4 slate. Gillispie was named Co-Southeastern Conference coach of the year along with Bruce Pearl of the Tennessee Volunteers.

73

Gillispie's Kentucky team opened the 2008–09 season with another loss at home, this time to the Virginia Military Institute, 103-111. However, on November 30, 2008, Gillispie led Kentucky to a 54–43 come –from-behind victory over West Virginia in the Findlay Toyota Las Vegas Invitational championship. Although his Wildcats had trailed for the entire game, Gillispie made halftime adjustments that stymied coach Bobby Huggins' Mountaineers, eventually allowing Kentucky to overcome a 14-point deficit well into the second half – holding the Mountaineers to only 17 second-half points. Although neither team was ranked, the win was considered an upset victory for Coach Gillispie and his Wildcats after the VMI loss .It was the first in-season tournament championship win for the University of Kentucky since winning the Great Alaska Shootout in late 1996.

After a 5–0 start in the SEC conference schedule, Gillispie's team dropped three straight games, to Ole Miss, South Carolina and Mississippi State , with the latter two losses coming at home. Some Kentucky fans vociferously booed Gillispie during the Mississippi State game. Kentucky rebounded against the Florida Gators with a 68–65 victory at home.

Kentucky went on to gain a 4th seed in the NIT, defeating UNLV, and Creighton in the opening and second rounds before losing to Notre Dame in the quarterfinals. Kentucky finished the year with an 8–8 record in conference play and 22–14 overall. The record tied for the second-most losses ever in the program's history.

John Calipari

John Calipari (2010-Now)

Kentucky Record: 123-23)

2009-10-- 35-3(NCAA Regional)
2010-11—29-9 (Final Four)
2011-12—38-2 (NCAA Champions)
2012-13—21-12 (NIT)

    The University of Kentucky named John Calipari as its 22nd basketball coach. April 2009, Calipari was the former head coach of the University of Memphis, the University of Massachusetts, and the National Basketball Association's New Jersey Nets.

    He is one of only two coaches (Rick Pitino) to direct three different colleges to a No. 1 seed in the NCAA Tournament, although two of those appearances (1996 at UMass and 2008 at Memphis) have been officially vacated by the NCAA. Calipari is also one of only two coaches to direct three different schools to a Final Four (1996– UMass, 2008– Memphis, 2011, 2012– Kentucky), with the UMass and Memphis appearances later being vacated by the NCAA. As a result, he is the only head coach to have a Final Four appearance vacated at more than one school, although Calipari himself was not personally implicated by the NCAA in either case. As a college coach, Calipari has 19 20-win seasons (18 official), 8 30-win seasons (7 official), and has been named National Coach of the Year 3 times.

In his first year as head coach, Calipari had a highly touted recruiting class, including the No. 1 overall rated recruit, John Wall, plus fellow 5-star recruits, Demarcus Cousins, Eric Bledsoe, and Daniel Orton. Kentucky won its 44th SEC Regular Season Championship in 2009–10, with a 14–2 conference record. Calipari's team followed this up with the UK's 26th SEC Tournament Championship, with an overtime defeat of Mississippi State, 75–74, in the SEC Tournament title game. In the NCAA Tournament; however, No. 1 seed Kentucky (East Region) was upset by West Virginia in the Elite 8, to finish the season at 35–3.

In his second season at Kentucky, Calipari recruited the No. 1 rated point guard in the 2010 class, Brandon Knight. In addition to Knight, Calipari also signed two other 5-star recruits, Terrence Jones and Doron Lamb. In 2010–11, Kentucky finished the regular season with a record of 22–8, with a 10–6 record in SEC regular season play. The Wildcats won their second consecutive SEC Tournament Championship, defeating Florida, 70–54, in the SEC Tournament title game. As a result, Kentucky received a No. 4 seed in the NCAA Tournament (East Regional). Rhey defeated No. 1 overall seed Ohio State, 62–60, in the Sweet-16. In the Elite Eight, Calipari's team avenged an early season loss to North Carolina, by defeating the Tar Heels, 76–69. That secured Kentucky's first Final Four appearance since 1998. In the Final Four, UK fell to the eventual NCAA Champions, U-Conn, by one point, 56–55, finishing with a final record of 29–9.

In his third season, Calipari landed another No. 1 recruiting class with four consensus five star players: Anthony Davis, Marquis Teague, Michael Kidd-Gilchrist, and Kyle Wiltjer. Kentucky came into the season ranked #2 in the country. They finished the regular season with a 30–1 record; their only loss was to Indiana by a buzzer-beater. They went 16–0 in conference play. In the SEC tournament, Kentucky lost in the championship game to Vanderbilt 71–64. In the NCAA Tournament, Calipari's team was selected as the overall #1 seed. Kentucky avenged the early season loss to Indiana; beating them in the Sweet Sixteen 102–90. They defeated Baylor in the Elite Eight 82–70, to advance to their second consecutive Final Four.

In New Orleans, they defeated Louisville, 69–61. Two days later, in the National Championship game, Kentucky played in another early season rematch against the Kansas Jayhawks, winning a hard fought contest 67–59. The win secured Calipari his first NCAA Championship, a NCAA record 38-win season, and the 8th overall NCAA Championship for Kentucky. By doing so, John Calipari became the 5th head coach to win a NCAA Championship at Kentucky (a NCAA record), and the first coach to do so at the school since 1998.

Following the 2012 championship, UK Athletics Director Mitch Barnhart announced on May 4 that Calipari's contract had been renegotiated. Under the new contract, Calipari would make $5.2M annually (not including bonuses), which further cemented his status as the most highly compensated college basketball coach in the country. Calipari earned almost $2M more per year than the second-most compensated coach in the country, Tom Izzo of Michigan State ($3.5M annually).

Michigan State's Tom Izzo and John Calipari on the recruiting trail.

Kentucky Assistant Coaches and Managers

Year	Coach	W	L	Assistant Coaches	Manager(s)
1902-03	WWH Mustaine	1	2	-	-
1903-04	Unnamed	1	4	-	Leander E. Andrus
1904-05	Unnamed	1	4		William Priest Kemper
1905-06	Unnamed	5	9	-	Wylie Brodbeck Wendt
1906-07	Unnamed	3	6	-	Augustus M. Kirby
1907-08	Unnamed	5	6	-	Leo Brewer
1908-09	Unnamed	5	4	-	James Floyd Chambers and

					Leonard C. Bridges
1909-10	Edwin R. Sweetland	4	8	Robert Hoover Spahr	Leonard C. Bridges
1910-11	Harold J. Iddings	5	6	-	Harvey Arthur Babb
1911-12	Edwin R. Sweetland	9	0	-	Giles Meadors
1912-13	John J. Tigert	5	3	-	W.C. Wilson
1913-14	Alpha Brumage	12	2	-	Wm. Tuttle
1914-15	Alpha Brumage	7	5	-	Abe Roth
1915-16	James Park	8	6	-	Armiel Carman
1916-17	William P. Tuttle	4	6	-	-
1917-18	Stanley A. Boles	9	2	-	-
1918-19	Andrew Gill	6	8	-	Ed Parker
1919-20	George C. Buchheit	5	7	-	-
1920-21	George C. Buchheit	13	1	-	-
1921-22	George C. Buchheit	10	6	-	-
1922-23	George C. Buchheit	3	10	-	Carl Riefkin
1923-24	George C.	13	3	-	-

	Buchheit				
1924-25	Clarence Applegran	13	8	-	-
1925-26	Ray Eklund	15	3	-	-
1926-27	Basil Hayden	3	13	-	-
1927-28	John Mauer	12	6	-	-
1928-29	John Mauer	12	5	-	William Griffeth
1929-30	John Mauer	16	3	-	Leonard Weakley
1930-31	Adolph Rupp	15	3	Cecil Combs, Birkette Pribble	Morris Levin
1931-32	Adolph Rupp	15	2	Len Miller	Robert Reynolds
1932-33	Adolph Rupp	21	3	Len Miller	Charles Maxson
1933-34	Adolph Rupp	16	1	Len Miller	Carey Burchett
1934-35	Adolph Rupp	19	2	Paul McBrayer	George Campbell, Jack May
1935-36	Adolph Rupp	15	6	Paul McBrayer	Jack May, Philip Haring, James McKenney
1936-37	Adolph Rupp	17	5	Paul McBrayer	James McKenney
1937-38	Adolph Rupp	13	5	Paul McBrayer	Philip Haring

1938-39	Adolph Rupp	16	4	Paul McBrayer	J.B. Faulconer
1939-40	Adolph Rupp	15	6	Paul McBrayer	Arthur Bicknell
1940-41	Adolph Rupp	17	8	Paul McBrayer	Garrett Fitzpatrick
1941-42	Adolph Rupp	19	6	Paul McBrayer	William Evans
1942-43	Adolph Rupp	17	6	Paul McBrayer	Bob Landrum
1943-44	Adolph Rupp	19	2	Harry Lancaster	Allan Abramson
1944-45	Adolph Rupp	22	4	Lyman Ginger	Harold Park
1945-46	Adolph Rupp	28	2	Elmer Gilb	Humzey Yessin
1946-47	Adolph Rupp	34	3	Harry Lancaster	Humzey Yessin
1947-48	Adolph Rupp	36	3	Harry Lancaster	Humzey Yessin
1948-49	Adolph Rupp	32	2	Harry Lancaster	Humzey Yessin
1949-50	Adolph Rupp	25	5	Harry Lancaster	Bobby Moore
1950-51	Adolph Rupp	32	2	Harry Lancaster	Bobby Moore
1951-52	Adolph Rupp	29	3	Harry Lancaster	Bobby Moore, Mike Dolan
1952-53		0	0	-	-
1953-54	Adolph Rupp	25	0	Harry Lancaster	Mike Dolan, George Perry

81

1954-55	Adolph Rupp	23	3	Harry Lancaster	Bill Surface
1955-56	Adolph Rupp	20	6	Harry Lancaster	Chigger Flynn, Ken Lehkamp
1956-57	Adolph Rupp	23	5	Harry Lancaster	Ken Lehkamp
1957-58	Adolph Rupp	23	6	Harry Lancaster, Bill Wireman	Jay Atkerson
1958-59	Adolph Rupp	24	3	Harry Lancaster, Dan Chandler	Jay Atkerson
1959-60	Adolph Rupp	18	7	Harry Lancaster	Tommy Thompson
1960-61	Adolph Rupp	19	9	Harry Lancaster, Doug Hines, Ted Lenhardt	Hunter Durham
1961-62	Adolph Rupp	23	3	Harry Lancaster, Ted Lenhardt, Jerry Gray	Hunter Durham
1962-63	Adolph Rupp	16	9	Harry Lancaster, Rudy Davalos, Ballard Moore, Neil Reed	Kirk Byers
1963-64	Adolph Rupp	21	6	Harry Lancaster, Neil Reed	Hub Metry, Doug Wolfe, Dan Omlar and Mike Harreld
1964-65	Adolph Rupp	15	10	Harry Lancaster, Neil	Hub Metry, Larry Crosby, Carson

				Reed, John Lykins	Harreld
1965-66	Adolph Rupp	27	2	Harry Lancaster, Joe B. Hall	Carson Harreld
1966-67	Adolph Rupp	13	13	Harry Lancaster, Joe B. Hall	Bobby Barton
1967-68	Adolph Rupp	22	5	Harry Lancaster, Joe B. Hall	Alan Theobald
1968-69	Adolph Rupp	23	5	Harry Lancaster, Joe B. Hall	Doug Billips
1969-70	Adolph Rupp	26	2	Joe B. Hall, T. L. Plain, Dick Parsons	Doug Billips, John McAdam
1970-71	Adolph Rupp	22	6	Joe B. Hall, T. L. Plain, Dick Parsons	John Ferguson
1971-72	Adolph Rupp	21	7	Joe B. Hall, W. Gale Catlett, Dick Parsons	John Ferguson
1972-73	Joe B. Hall	20	8	Dick Parsons, Boyd Grant, Jim Hatfield, Ken Trivette	Glenn Sims
1973-74	Joe B. Hall	13	13	Dick Parsons, Boyd Grant, Jim Hatfield, Jim Dinwiddie, Ken Trivette	Don Adkins

1974-75	Joe B. Hall	26	5	Dick Parsons, Leonard Hamilton, Lynn Nance, Ray Edelman	-Don Adkns
1975-76	Joe B. Hall	20	10	Dick Parsons, Leonard Hamilton, Lynn Nance	Tripp Ramsey
1976-77	Joe B. Hall	26	4	Dick Parsons, Leonard Hamilton, Jim Long, Jim Andrews	Tripp Ramsey
1977-78	Joe B. Hall	30	2	Dick Parsons, Leonard Hamilton, Joe Dean Jr., Frank Ramsey	Don Sullivan
1978-79	Joe B. Hall	19	12	Dick Parsons, Leonard Hamilton, Joe Dean Jr.	Don Sullivan
1979-80	Joe B. Hall	29	6	Dick Parsons, Leonard Hamilton, Joe Dean Jr., Jim Lankster	George Fletcher
1980-81	Joe B. Hall	22	6	Leonard Hamilton, Joe Dean Jr., Bob Chambers, Harry Lancaster	George Fletcher

1981-82	Joe B. Hall	22	8	Leonard Hamilton, Joe Dean Jr., Bob Chambers, Gordy Parido	Roger Thomas
1982-83	Joe B. Hall	23	8	Leonard Hamilton, Joe Dean Jr., Bob Chambers, Jeff Riley	Roger Thomas
1983-84	Joe B. Hall	29	5	Leonard Hamilton, Jim Hatfield, Lake Kelly, Wayne Breeden	Randy Azbill
1984-85	Joe B. Hall	18	13	Leonard Hamilton, Jim Hatfield, Lake Kelly	Randy Azbill
1985-86	Eddie Sutton	32	4	Leonard Hamilton, James Dickey, Doug Barnes, Wayne Breeden	-
1986-87	Eddie Sutton	18	11	James Dickey, Dwane Casey, Doug Barnes, Wayne Breeden	-
1987-88	Eddie Sutton	27	6	James Dickey, Dwane Casey, Jimmy Dykes, Roger Harden	-

1988-89	Eddie Sutton	13	19	James Dickey, Dwane Casey, Jimmy Dykes, Brock Touloukian	David Deaton, Robert Gayheart, Jeff Kidder, Eric Moore, Jeff Morroww, Spencer Tatum, Elki Umezaki
1989-90	Rick Pitino	14	14	Ralph Willard, Orlando Smith, Herb Sendek, Billy Donovan	Kenneth Gayheart, Jeff Morrow, Spencer Tatum
1990-91	Rick Pitino	22	6	Orlando Smith, Herb Sendek, Billy Donovan, Bernadette Locke	Kenneth Gayheart, Jeff Morrow, Spencer Tatum, Vincent Tatum
1991-92	Rick Pitino	29	7	Herb Sendek, Billy Donovan, Bernadette Locke-Mattox, Mike Atkinson	John Farris, Kenneth Gayheart, Jeff Morrow, Spencer Tatum, Vincent Tatum
1992-93	Rick Pitino	30	4	Herb Sendek, Billy Donovan, Bernadette Locke-Mattox	Spencer Tatum, John Farris
1993-94	Rick Pitino	27	7	Billy Donovan, Delray Brooks, Bernadette Locke-Mattox	John Farris, Kenneth Gayheart, Sean Gray, Tony Russell, Brian Stocker
1994-95	Rick Pitino	28	5	Jim O'Brien, Delray Brooks, Winston Bennett	John Farris, Sean Gray, Tony Russell, Brian Stocker

1995-96	Rick Pitino	34	2	Jim O'Brien, Delray Brooks, Winston Bennett	J. David Bolen, Zach Goines, Sean Gray, Mike Howard, Tony Russell, Brian Stocker, Frank Vogel
1996-97	Rick Pitino	35	5	Jim O'Brien, Delray Brooks, Winston Bennett	Sean Alteri, J. David Bolen, Zach Goines, Sean Gray, Mike Howard, Tony Russell, Brian Stocker
1997-98	Orlando Smith	35	4	George Felton, Shawn Finney, Mike Sutton	J. David Bolen, Zach Goines, Aaron Howard, Mike Howard, Dan McHale, Jason Seamonds, Anthony Summers
1998-99	Orlando Smith	28	9	George Felton, Shawn Finney, Mike Sutton	Zach Goines, Aaron Howard, Dan McHale, Jason Seaman's, Anthony Summers
1999-00	Orlando Smith	23	10	George Felton, Shawn Finney, Mike Sutton	Aaron Howard, David Judy, Dan McHale, Caleb Moore, Anthony Summers
2000-01	Orlando Smith	24	10	Mike Sutton, David Hobbs, Reggie Hanson	D.J. Geddes, Aaron Howard, David Judy, Dan

					McHale, Caleb Moore
2001-02	Orlando Smith	22	10	Mike Sutton, David Hobbs, Reggie Hanson	D.J. Geddes, Steve Goodson, Aaron Howard, David Judy, Caleb Moore
2002-03	Orlando Smith	32	4	David Hobbs, Reggie Hanson, Scott Rigot	Allen Edwards, D.J. Geddes, Steve Goodson, Danny Jett, Caleb Moore
2003-04	Orlando Smith	27	5	David Hobbs, Reggie Hanson, Scott Rigot	Jeremiah Cox, D.J. Geddes, Steve Goodson
2004-05	Orlando Smith	28	6	David Hobbs, Reggie Hanson, Scott Rigot	Chris Briggs, Jeremiah Cox, D.J. Geddes, Steve Goodson, Jonathan Morris, Zach Murphy
2005-06	Orlando Smith	22	13	David Hobbs, Reggie Hanson, Scott Rigot	Chris Briggs, Jeremiah Cox, A.J. Davis, Will Herschelman, Dustin Marr, Zach Murphy, Brad Noe, Doug Smith
2006-07	Orlando Smith	22	12	David Hobbs, Reggie Hanson, Scott Rigot	Chris Briggs, Will Campbell, Jeremy French, Will Herschelman, Dustin Marr, Luke Mason, Zach Murphy, Chad

					Sanders
2007-08	Billy Gillispie	18	13	Glynn Cyprien, Jeremy Cox, Tracy Webster	Craig Callihan, Will Campbell, Jeremy French, Will Herschelman, Dustin Marr, Luke Mason, Zach Murphy, Chad Sanders
2008-09	Billy Gillispie	22	14	Glynn Cyprien, Jeremy Cox, Tracy Webster	Craig Callahan, Will Campbell, Jeremy French, Will Herschelman, Andrew Rogers, Chad Sanders
2009-10	John Calipari	35	3	Orlando Antigua, John Robic, Rod Strickland	- Chris Briggs, Will Campbell, Jeremy French, Will Herschelman, Dustin Marr, Luke Mason, Zach Murphy, Chad Sanders Craig Callihan, Will Campbell, Jeremy French, Will Herschelman, Dustin Marr, Luke Mason, Zach Murphy, Chad Sanders
2010-11	John Calipari	29	9	Orlando Antigua, John	- Craig Callihan, Will Campbell,

				Robic, Kenny Payne	Jeremy French, Will Herschelman, Dustin Marr, Luke Mason, Zach Murphy, Chad Sanders
2011-12	John Calipari	38	2	Orlando Antigua, Kenny Payne, John Robic	- Craig Callihan, Will Campbell, Jeremy French, Will Herschelman, Andrew Rogers, Chad Sanders
2012-2013	John Calipari	21	12	Orlando Antigua, Kenny Payne, John Robic	- Matt Evans, Blake Perkins, Robert Hatchett, Bo Rodriquez, Andrew Ortell, Will Barton

Chapter Six
UK Basketball Hall of Fame

Cliff Barker

Cliff Barker (1947-48, 49)

Hometown: Yorktown, Ind. (High)
Position: G-F Playing Height: 6-2 Playing Weight: 185
Date of Birth: January 15, 1921
Date of Death: March 17, 1998
Kentucky Career Notes:
Olympic Champion
Retired Jersey #23
Season Notes:
1947-48: All-SEC [Second Team]; All-SEC Tournament
1948-49: All-SEC [Second Team (AP)]; All-SEC Tournament
Post-UK Career Notes:
Served in the Military

Drafted in the 1949 NBA Draft by Indianapolis

Ralph Beard

Ralph Beard, G (1946, 47 48, 49)

Position: G, Height: 5' 10" Weight: 175
Hometown: Louisville, KY (Male)
Date of Birth: December 2, 1927 (Hardinsburg)
Date of Death: November 29, 2007
Legal Name: Milton M. Beard
Kentucky Career Notes:
Olympic Champion
Retired Jersey #12
Multi-Sport Player [Football and Baseball]
Season Notes:
1945-46: All-SEC [First Team]; All-SEC Tournament
1946-47: All-American [Consensus (1st), NABC (1st), Converse
(1st), True Magazine (1st), Helms (1st)]; All-SEC [First Team];
All-SEC Tournament

1947-48: All-American [Consensus (1st), AP (1st), NABC (1st), Converse (1st), True Magazine (1st), Helms (1st)]; All-SEC [First Team]; All-SEC Tournament
1948-49: All-American [Consensus (1st), AP (1st), UPI (1st), NABC (1st), Converse (2nd), Helms, Look (2nd), Sporting News (3rd), Colliers (1st)]; All-SEC [First Team (AP)]; All-SEC Tournament
Post-UK Career Notes:
Served in the Military
Drafted in the 2nd Round of the 1949 NBA Draft by Chicago

Jerry Bird

Jerry Bird (C/F) (1954, 55, 56)

Hometown: Corbin, KY
Position: F Playing Height: 6-6 Playing Weight: 200
Date of Birth: February 2, 1935 [
Prep Notes:

Chuck Taylor and North-South All-Star
Kentucky Career Notes:
Retired Jersey #22
Season Notes:
1955-56: (All-SEC Second Team (AP & Coaches)
Post-UK Career Notes:
Drafted in the 1956 NBA Draft by Minneapolis

Sam Bowie

Sam Bowie (1980, 84)

Hometown: Lebanon, PA (High)
Position: C-F Height: 7-1 Weight: 230
Nickname: "Boo"
Olympian
Retired Jersey #31
pts., 13.4 ppg
Rebounds: (7th.) 843, 8.8 rpg
Season Notes:

1979-80: All-SEC; All-SEC Tournament
1980-81: All-American [Consensus (2nd)]; First Team All-SEC)
1981-82: (Did not play – medical redshirt)
1982-83: (Did not play - medical redshirt)
1983-84: All-American [AP (2nd), Sporting News (2nd)]; All-NCAA Regional Team;

Bob Burrow

Bob Burrow (1955, 56)

Hometown: Wells, TX (High)
Position: C Playing Height: 6-7 Playing Weight: 215
Date of Birth: June 29, 1934
Legal Name: Robert Brantley Burrow
Game by Game Statistics
Kentucky Career Notes:
Retired Jersey #50

Transferred from Lon Morris (TX) Junior College
Season Notes:
1954-55: All-American [AP (3rd), Helms (2nd)]; All- NCAA
Regional Team; All-SEC [First Team (AP)]
1955-56: All-American [Consensus (2nd), AP (3rd), UPI (3rd),
NABC (1st), Converse (2nd), Look (1st), Colliers (2nd),
Newspaper Enterprise Assn. (2nd), Helms (2nd)]; All- NCAA
Regional Team; All-SEC [First Team (AP & Coaches)]
Post-UK Career Notes:
Drafted in the 1956 NBA Draft by Rochester

Burgess Carey

Burgess Carey (1925, 26)

Hometown: Lexington, KY (Senior)
Position: G Playing Height: 6-0 Playing Weight: 195
Date of Birth: March 4, 1905
Date of Death: December 2, 1961
Prep Notes:

National High School Basketball Interscholastic All-American
Kentucky Career Notes:
Transferred from Washington & Lee
Season Notes:
1924-25: All-American [Helms]

Mike Casey (1968, 69, 71)

Mike Casey

Hometown: Simpsonville, KY (Shelby County)
Position: G Playing Height: 6-4 Playing Weight: 187
Date of Birth: May 26, 1948
Date of Death: April 9, 2009
Prep Notes:
Mr. Basketball State of Kentucky 1966
Scholastic Coach All-American
Season Notes:
1967-68: All- NCAA Regional Team; All-SEC [First Team (AP,
UPI & Coaches)]

1968-69: All-SEC [First Team (Coaches) Second Team (AP & UPI)]
1970-71: All-SEC [First Team (UPI) Second Team (AP)]; Academic All-American; Academic All-SEC
Post-UK Career Notes:
Drafted #130 Overall in the 8th Round of the 1970 NBA Draft by Chicago

Rex Chapman

Rex Chapman (1986, 87)

Hometown: Owensboro, KY (Apollo)
Position: G Playing Height: 6-5 Playing Weight: 185
Date of Birth: October 5, 1967
Prep Notes:
Mr. Basketball State of Kentucky 1986
Gatorade State Player of Year
Parade All-American
Scholastic Coach All-American
McDonalds All-American Kentucky
Career Notes:
Declared Early for NBA Draft after Sophomore Season

Left for Professional Basketball after Sophomore Season for NBA.

Season Notes: Before turning pro after his sophomore year Chapman was en route to rivaling Kyle Macy as the most popular Wildcat ever. He got off to a rousing start, debuting with an18-point performance against Austin Peay; a month later he scored 26 points against Louisville in Freedom Hall. The "Boy King" bowed out with a 30-point performance against Louisville in an NCAA game.

Single Game Highs: Points: 30: Rebounds: 7; Assists: 8; Field Goals: 12; FGA's: 22; Free Throws: 7; FTA's: 8; 3 pt Field Goals: 6; Steals: 5; Blocked Shots: 3: Minutes: 41

 Career Scoring: (43rd) 1,073 pts, 17.6 ppg. Before turning pro after his sophomore year Chapman was en route to rivaling Kyle Macy as the most popular Wildcat ever.

1986-87: All-SEC [First Team (Coaches)]; All-SEC Freshman Team

1987-88: All-American [NABC (3rd), Basketball Times (3rd)]; All-SEC [First Team (AP, UPI & Coaches)]; SEC Tournament MVP; Academic All-SEC

Post-UK Career Notes:

Drafted #8 Overall in the 1st Round of the 1988 NBA Draft by Charlotte

Nickname: "King" Rex

Larry Conley

Larry Conley (1964, 65, 66)

Hometown: Ashland, KY (High)
Position: F-C Playing Height: 6-3 Playing Weight: 172
Date of Birth: January 22, 1944
Game by Game Statistics
Prep Notes:
Scholastic Coach All-American
Kentucky Career Notes:
Multi-Sport Player [Baseball]
Season Notes:
1963-64: All-SEC [Third Team (AP)]; Academic All-American;
Academic All-SEC
1964-65: All-SEC [Third Team]; Academic All-SEC
1965-66: All-SEC [First Team (Coaches) Third Team (AP &
UPI)]
Post-UK Career Notes:

Served in the Military.

Johnny Cox

Johnny Cox (1957, 58), 59)

Hometown: Hazard, KY High
Position: F Playing Height: 6-4 Playing Weight: 185
Date of Birth: November 1, 1936
Kentucky Career Notes:
Retired Jersey #24
Cox was drafted #37 Overall in the 4th Round of the 1958 NBA
Draft by New York (Junior-Eligible)
Season Notes:
1956-57: All-American [UPI (3rd), Helms (3rd)]; All- NCAA
Regional Team; All-SEC [First Team (AP & Coaches)]
1957-58: All-NCAA Final Four Team; All- NCAA Regional
Team; All-SEC [First Team (Coaches) Second Team (AP)]
1958-59: All-American [Consensus (1st), AP (1st), UPI (2nd),
NABC (1st), USBWA (1st), Converse (1st), Helms (1st),

Sporting News (2nd), Look Magazine (1st), Newspaper
Enterprises Assn. (2nd)]; All- NCAA Regional Team; All-SEC
[First Team (AP & Coaches]
Post- UK Career Notes:
Drafted #30 Overall in the 4th Round of the 1959 NBA Draft by
New York

Louie Dampier

Louie Dampier (1965, '66, '67)

Hometown: Indianapolis, IN (Southport High)
Position: G Height: 6-0 Weight: 167
Date of Birth: November 20, 1944
Retired Jersey #10
Multi-Sport Player [Baseball]
Season Notes:
1964-65: All-SEC
1965-66: All-American [Consensus]; All-NCAA Final Four
Team; All- NCAA Regional Team; Academic All-SEC

1966-67: All-American [Consensus]; All-SEC; Academic All-American; Academic All-SEC

Tony Delk

Tony Delk (1993, '94, '95, '96)

Hometown: Brownsville, TN (Haywood)
Position: G, Height: 6-1 Weight: 193
Date of Birth: January 28, 1974
Season Notes:
Delk led the team for the third consecutive year in scoring (17.8). He tied an NCAA record with seven three's in the 1996 win over Syracuse. His 1,890 points rank sixth on UK's all-time scorer's list. Delk is UK's leader in treys (283 in 712 attempts), making at least one three in 34 consecutive games.
Single Game Highs: Points: 31, Rebounds, 10; Assists, 5, Field Goals: 11; |FGA's: 23); 3 pt FG's: 9; 3 pt FGA's; Blocked Shots: 3 Scoring: (5th.) 1,890 pts., 14.2 ppg (1st.),* 283 of 712 (*UK Record) Game: 9 treys

1993-94: Second Team All-SEC; All-SEC Tournament
1994-95: All- NCAA Regional Team; All-SEC
1995-96: All-American [Consensus]; NCAA Final Four MOP;
NCAA Regional MOP; SEC Player of the Year; All-SEC
Postgame: rafted o. 16 overall by Charlotte.

John DeMoisey

John DeMoisey (1935)

Hometown: Walton, KY (High)
Position: C-F Playing Height: 6-4 Playing Weight: 170
Date of Death: August 1, 1963
Nickname: "Frenchy"
Kentucky Career Notes:
Retired Jersey #00
Multi-Sport Player [Baseball]
Brother of Kentucky player Truett DeMoisey and son-in-law of
former Kentucky player H.H. Downing
Season Notes:
1931-32: (Ineligible part of year due to academics)

1932-33: All-SEC [First Team]; All-SEC Tournament
1933-34: All-American [Helms]; All-SEC [First Team]; All-SEC Tournament

Leroy Edwards

Leroy Edwards (1934-35)

Hometown: Indianapolis, IN (Arsenal Tech)
Position: C Playing Height: 6-4 Playing Weight: 215
Date of Birth: April 11, 1914
Date of Death: August 25, 1971
Nickname: Leroy "Cowboy" Edwards
Kentucky Career Notes:
Left for Professional Basketball after Sophomore Season for Industrial League in Indiana
Season Notes:

1934-35: National Player of the Year [Helms]; All-American [Consensus (1st), Helms, Converse (2nd)]; All-SEC [First Team]
Post-UK Career Notes:
Mr. Edwards passed up his junior year to join the Oshkosh (Wis.) All Stars in the National Professional Basketball League, a forerunner of the National Basketball Association.
He played for the team from 1936 through 1942 and was all-league center from 1938-42. He led the NPBL in scoring in 1938, 1939 and 1940. He also owned an Oshkosh tavern during most of his time with the team

Billy Evans

Billy Evans (1952, 54, 55)

Hometown: Berea, KY
Position: F/G Playing Height: 6-1 Playing Weight: 170
Kentucky Career Notes:
Olympic Champion
Retired Jersey #42
Multi-Sport Player [Tennis and Baseball]
Season Notes:
1954-55: All-SEC [Third Team (AP)]
Post-UK Career Notes:
Drafted in the 1955 NBA Draft by Rochester

Richard Farmer

Richard Farmer (1989, 90, 91, 92)

Hometown: Manchester, KY (Clay County)
Position: G Playing Height: 6-0 Playing Weight: 170
Date of Birth: August 25, 1969
Legal Name: Richard Dwight Farmer
Nickname:" Richie"
Prep Notes:
Mr. Basketball State of Kentucky 1988
Gatorade State Player of Year

Jack "Goose" Givens

Jack "Goose" Givens (1995, 96, 97, 98)

Hometown: Lexington, KY (Bryan Station)
Position: F Playing Height: 6-4 Playing Weight: 205
Date of Birth: September 21, 1956
Nickname: "Goose"
Prep Notes:
Mr. Basketball State of Kentucky 1974
Parade All-American
Scholastic Coach All-American
Kentucky Career Notes:
Retired Jersey #21
Season Notes:
1975-76: All-American [Helms]; All-SEC [First Team (Coaches)
Second Team (AP & UPI)
1976-77: All-American [NABC (4th), Helms]; All- NCAA
Regional Team; All-SEC [First Team (AP, UPI & Coaches)]

1977-78: National Player of the Year [Helms]; All-American Consensus (2nd), AP (2nd), UPI (2nd), NABC (2nd), USBWA (2nd), Converse (1st), Helms, Wooden (1st)]; NCAA Final Four Most Outstanding Player; NCAA Regional Most Outstanding Player; All-SEC [First Team (AP, UPI & Coaches)
Post-UK Career Notes:
Drafted #16 overall by Atlanta.
Jack Givens is remembered mainly because of his 41-point performance against Duke in the 1978 NCAA championship game. Givens was known as "Mr. Slick" and James Lee was "Mr. Steel" in Lexington high school circles. While Givens was a three-year starter at UK, Lee was a valuable sixth man who also drew some starting assignments. James isn't among the top 20 on the list, but he can fill his name in Rupp's open spot.

Phil Grawemeyer

Phil Grawemeyer (`1954, 55, 56)

Hometown: Louisville, KY (Manual)

Position: F Playing Height: 6-7 Playing Weight: 180
Date of Death: March 20, 2008 [Marquette - 66 - 74]
Nickname "Cookie"
Prep Notes:
North-South All-Star
Kentucky Career Notes:
Retired Jersey #44
Multi-Sport Player [Baseball]
Post-UK Career Notes:
Drafted in the 1956 NBA Draft by Minneapolis

Kevin Grevey

Kevin Grevey (1973, '74. '75)

Hometown: Hamilton, OH Taft
Position: F Height: 6-5 Weight: 205
Date of Birth: May 12, 1953

UK Career
Single Game Highs: Points: 40; | Retired Jersey #35
　　　Grevey hit 51.7 percent of his field goal attempts at UK.
He led the Wildcats in scoring his junior and senior years
Field Goals: 17; FGA's: 30; Free Throws: 12; Free Throw
Attempts: 12.|
Career Scoring: (7th), 1801 pts., 21.4 ppg
Rebounds: 547, 6.5 rpg.
Season Notes:
1972-73: SEC Player of the Year
1973-74: All-American
1974-75: All-American [Consensus)]; All-NCAA Final Four
Team; All-SEC

Vernon Hatton

Vernon Hatton (1956, 57, 58)

Hometown: Lexington, KY (Lafayette)
Position: G Height: 6-3 Weight: 195
Date of Birth: January 13, 1936
Retired Jersey #52

Hatton was one of the best clutch players in UK history. He is remembered most for a UK three-overtime win against Temple. In a 1958 UK win over Temple, Vernon sank a 47-foot shot as time expired to force a second overtime; then he scored UK's last eight points in the third overtime. In the national semifinals Hatton scored a lay-up with 16 seconds remaining that gave UK a 61-60 victory over the Owls. He scored 30 points in an 84-72 win over Seattle in the championship game.
Single Game Highs: Field Goals: 16; Free Throws: 12; Points: 35
Career Scoring: (39th.), 1,153 pts, 15.2 ppg
Season Notes:
1957-58: All-American; All-NCAA Final Four Team; All-NCAA Regional Team; All-SEC

Wallace Jones

Wallace Jones (1946, '47, '48, '49)

Hometown: Harlan, KY High
Position: F-C Height: 6-4 Weight: 205
Date of Birth: July 14, 1926

Nickname: "Wah Wah"
Olympic Champion
Retired Jersey #27
Multi-Sport Player [Football and Baseball]
Jones earned a total of 11 UK varsity letters—four each in basketball and football and three in baseball, which makes him the all-time varsity letter winner at UK. He lost his final year of eligibility in baseball when senior members of the 1949 NCAA champions went on tour.
Single Game Highs: Field Goals: 10; - | |
Free Throws: 6;| Points: 22
Career Scoring: (40th.), 1,151 pts, 9.1 ppg
Season Notes:
1945-46: First Team All-SEC; All-SEC Tournament
1946-47: All-American [Converse (2nd)]; First Team All-SEC; All-SEC Tournament
1947-48: All-American [Converse (3rd)]; First Team All-SEC; All-SEC Tournament

Kyle Macy

Kyle Macy (1978, '79, '80)

Hometown: Peru, IN High
Position: G, Height: 6-3, Weight: 180
Date of Birth: April 9, 1957
Retired Jersey No. 4

Macy was perhaps the most popular player ever to wear the Blue & White. After transferring from Purdue, he laid out a year and as a sophomore was floor leader of the 1978 NCAA champions. The fans adored him, the coaches appreciated him, and his teammates respected him. He was unflappable in tight situations, as evidenced by his school record .890 from the line.

Kyle Macy arguably was the most popular basketball player ever to wear the UK Blue & White. There was so much demand for autographs, pictures and other mementos that go with celebrity that the Sports Information Office assigned a special secretary to the task. Students clamored to attend his student teaching classes at a local high school. Parents named their newborns after him. Boys in the sandlots mimicked his habit of drying his hands on his socks before shooting a free throw.

The All-America guard was unflappable through it all. He went about his business as usual; never a hair out of place and his face sometimes an inscrutable mask. The hair is mostly gone now and sometimes the Morehead State team that Macy coached played in Rupp Arena, where he always receives a warm welcome. Single Game Highs: Points: 32, Rebounds: 7; Assists: 10; Field Goals: 13; FGA; 21; Free. Throws: 12; - | FTA's: 12.|
Career Scoring: (19th.) 1,411 pts. (14.4 ppg)
Free Throws: 331/372 (89.0%-UK Record)
Assists: (6th.) 470
Season Highlights
All-American [UPI (3rd)]; NCAA Regional Most Outstanding Player;

1978-79: All-American [Converse (2nd), All-SEC Tournament; Academic All-American; Academic All-SEC
1979-80 All-American [Consensus]; All-SEC
SEC Player of the Year

Tayshaun Prince

Tayshaun Prince (1999, 2000, 2001, 2002)

Hometown: Compton, CA Dominguez
Position: G/F Height: 6-9 Weight: 213
Date of Birth: February 28, 1980
     Prince led UK scorers (13.3 ppg) as a sophomore, averaged 16.1 as a junior and ended his UK career with a team-leading 17.5 and 6.3 scoring and rebounding averages. His 1,775 points total ranks seventh on UK's list of leading scorers.
     Single Game Highs: Points: 41; Rebounds: 12; Assists: 7; Field Goals: 14; FGAs: 22; Free Throws: 11; FTAs: 12; 3 pt Field Goals: 7; 3 pt FGAs: 11; Steals: 4; Blocked Shots. Career Scoring: (8th.) 1,775 pts., Rebounds: 749

Assists: 255; Blocked shots: (7th.) 142
Season Notes:
1999-00: Second Team All-SEC
2000-01: All-American,), SEC Player of the Year; All-SEC; SEC
Tournament MVP
2001-02: All-American; All- NCAA Regional Team

Pat Riley

Pat Riley (65, 66, 67)

Hometown: Schenectady, NY (Linton High)
Position: F Playing Height: 6-4 Playing Weight: 205
Date of Birth: March 20, 1945
Prep Notes:
Scholastic Coach All-American
Kentucky Career Notes:
Retired Jersey #42
Future NBA Championship Coach

Season Notes:
1965-66: All-American [AP (3rd), UPI (3rd), USBWA (1st), Converse (2nd), Helms]; All-NCAA Final Four Team; NCAA Regional Most Outstanding Player; SEC Player of the Year [Associated Press] ; All-SEC [First Team (AP, UPI & Coaches)]
1966-67: All-SEC [First Team (Coaches) Second Team (AP & UPI)]
Post-UK Career Notes:
Basketball Hall of Fame
Drafted #7 Overall in the 1st Round of the 1967 NBA Draft by San Diego

Rick Robey

Rick Robey (1976, 77, 78)

Hometown: New Orleans, LA (Brother Martin High)
Position: F-C Playing Height: 6-10 Playing Weight: 235
Date of Birth: January 30, 1956 [Georgia Tech - 84 - 62]
Nickname: Rick

Prep Notes:

Mr. Basketball State of Louisiana 1974 (AP)

Parade All-American

Scholastic Coach All-American

Kentucky Career Notes:

Retired Jersey #53

Season Notes:

1974-75: All-SEC [Third Team (AP)]

1976-77: All-American [NABC (4th), Converse (1st)]; All-SEC [First Team (AP, UPI & Coaches)]

1977-78: All-American [Consensus (2nd), AP (3rd), UPI (2nd), NABC (1st), Converse (1st), Sporting News (2nd), Wooden (1st), Helms]; All-NCAA Final Four Team; All-SEC [First Team (AP, UPI & Coaches)]

Post-UK Career Notes:

Drafted #3 Overall in the 1st Round of the 1978 NBA Draft by Indiana

Kenny Rollins

Kenny Rollins (1946 47, 48)

118

Hometown: Wickliffe, KY
Position: G Playing Height: 6-0 Playing Weight: 175
Date of Birth: July 14, 1923
Date of Death: October 9, 2012
Kentucky Career Notes:
Olympic Champion
Retired Jersey #26
Season Notes:
1946-47: All-SEC [First Team]; All-SEC Tournament
1947-48: All-SEC [First Team]; All-SEC Tournament
Post-UK Career Notes:
Served in the Military
Drafted in the 1948 NBA Draft by Fort Wayne

Gayle Rose

Gayle Rose (1952, 54, 55)

Hometown: Paris, KY
Position: G Playing Height: 6-0 Playing Weight: 170
Date of Birth: November 2, 1932

Prep Notes:
Chuck Taylor Player of Year and North-South All-Star
Kentucky Career Notes:
Retired Jersey #20

Layton Rouse

Layton Rouse (1938, 39, 40)

Hometown: Ludlow, KY
Position: G Playing Height: 6-1 Playing Weight: 169
Date of Birth: May 11, 1918
Date of Death: April 14, 2012
Nickname: L "Mickey"
Kentucky Career Notes:
Retired Jersey #10
Season Notes:
1939-40: All-SEC [First Team]; All-SEC Tournament

Post-UK Career Notes:
Served in the Military

Forest Sale

Forest Sale (1931, 32, 33)

Hometown: Harrodsburg, KY (Kavanaugh)
Position: C-F Playing Height: 6-4
Date of Birth: June 25, 1911
Date of Death: December 4, 1985
Nickname: "Aggie" Sale (More)
Kentucky Career Notes:
Retired Jersey #19
Season Notes:
1931-32: All-American [Consensus (1st), Converse (1st), Helms,
College Humor (1st)]
1932-33: National Player of the Year [Helms]; All-American
[Consensus (1st), Converse (1st), College Humor (1st), Helms];
All-SEC [First Team]; All-SEC Tournament

Post-UK Career Notes:
Served in the Military

Carey Spicer

Carey Spicer (1929, 30, 31)

Hometown: Lexington, KY (Senior)
Position: F Playing Height: 6-1
Date of Birth: April 23, 1909
Date of Death: December 5, 1996
Kentucky Career Notes:
Retired Jersey #17
Multi-Sport Player [Football and Tennis]
Brother of future Kentucky player Bill Spicer and brother-in-law
of future Kentucky player Elmer Gilb
Season Notes:
1928-29: All-American [Helms]; All-Southern Conference
1929-30: All-Southern Conference
1930-31: All-American [Helms]; All-Southern Conference

Post-UK Career Notes: Spicer was the first two-time basketball All-American at UK, and the first All-American player under legendary coach Adolph Rupp.

Spicer set records in UK football that stood for 40 years. A quarterback on the 1928, 1929, and 1930 teams, Mr. Spicer set records for most touchdowns - 11 - and most points - 75 - in a season. He also was a top-flight tennis player and ran track at UK.

In 1964 he became the second former UK player to be elected into the Helms Basketball Hall of Fame.
Served in the military.

William "Grits" Spivey

William "Grits" Spivey (1950, 51)

Hometown: Warner Robins, GA (Macon Jordan}
Position: C Height: 7-0 Weight: 230
Date of Birth: March 19, 1929

Spivey led Wildcat scoring both his varsity years and averaged 17.0 rebounds with the 1951 NCAA championship team. He probably would have ranked alongside Issel if he had played his senior season.

When Bill Spivey attended a UK basketball tryout in the summer of 1948, Rupp said, "His seven feet is interesting, but to tell the truth, he doesn't look like very much. He is scrawny (6'10 1/2", 170 lbs.), he lacks coordination, he is awkward, he doesn't have any shots, and he stands around flat-footed. However, he can run fairly fast, and he seems sincere and very intent in his desire to play for us."

Single Game Bests: Field Goals: 16; Free Throws: 9; FTA's: 13; Points: 40

Scoring; (34th.) 1,213 pts., 19.3 ppg.

Rebounds: Season - 567 – UK Record

Season Notes:

1949-50: All-American (3rd.), All-SEC; All-SEC Tournament

1950-51: All-American [Consensus]; All-NCAA Final Four Team; All- NCAA Regional Team; All-SEC ; All-SEC Tournament

Retired Jersey #77

Adrian Smith

Adrian Smith (1956, 57, 58)

Hometown: Farmington, KY
Position: G Playing Height: 6-0 Playing Weight: 178
Date of Birth: October 5, 1936
Nickname: "Odie"
Kentucky Career Notes:
Olympic Champion
Transferred from Northeast Mississippi Junior College
Post-UK Career Notes:
Served in the Military
Basketball Hall of Fame
Drafted #86 Overall in the 15th Round of the 1958 NBA Draft
by Cincinnati

Lou Tsioropoulos

Lou Tsioropoulos (1951, 52--54)

Hometown: Lynn, MA (Classic)
Position: F Playing Height: 6-5 Playing Weight: 200
Date of Birth: August 31, 1930
Kentucky Career Notes:
Retired Jersey #16
Multi-Sport Player [Football]
Season Notes:
1953-54: All-SEC [Second Team (AP)]
Post-UK Career Notes:
Served in the Military
Drafted #24 Overall in the 7th Round of the 1953 NBA Draft by
Boston

Kenny Walker

Kenny Walker (1983, 84, 85, 86)

Hometown: Roberta, GA (Crawford County Comprehensive)
Position: F Playing Height: 6-8 Playing Weight: 190
Date of Birth: August 18, 1964
Nickname "Sky"
Game by Game Statistics
Prep Notes:
Mr. Basketball State of Georgia 1982
Parade All-American
Scholastic Coach All-American
McDonalds All-American
Kentucky Career Notes:
Retired Jersey #34
Season Notes:
1982-83: All-SEC [Third Team (AP)]

1983-84: All-SEC [First Team (Coaches) Second Team (AP) Third Team (UPI)]

1984-85: All-American [Consensus (2nd), AP (2nd), UPI (2nd), NABC (2nd), USBWA (2nd), Basketball Times (2nd), Wooden (1st)]; All- NCAA Regional Team; SEC Player of the Year [Associated Press & United Press International]; All-SEC [First Team (AP, UPI & Coaches)]

1985-86: All-American [Consensus (1st), AP (1st), UPI (1st), NABC (1st), USBWA (1st), Sporting News (2nd), Basketball Times (1st), Wooden (1st)]; All- NCAA Regional Team; SEC Player of the Year [Associated Press & United Press International]; All-SEC [First Team (AP, UPI & Coaches)]

Post-UK Career Notes:

Drafted #5 Overall in the 1st Round of the 1986 NBA Draft by New York

Sean Woods

Sean Woods (1990, 91, 92)

Hometown: Indianapolis, IN (Cathedral)
Position: G Playing Height: 6-2 Playing Weight: 180
Date of Birth: March 29, 1970
Kentucky Career Notes:
Retired Jersey #11

Season Notes:
1988-89: (Did not play - Ineligible)
1991-92: All- NCAA Regional Team

Biggest Shots

Ralph Beard
Mar.20, 1946 vs. Rhode Island
This free throw with 43 seconds left gave Adolph Rupp his first national title, 46-45.

Ralph Beard
Feb. 14, 1948 vs. Tennessee
The buzzer-beater is still one of the longest shots (52.5') in UK history.

Vernon Hatton
Dec. 7, 1957 vs. Temple
Hatton's 47-foot bomb from midcourt tied the game at the end of the first overtime.

Terry Mobley
Dec. 31, 1963 vs. Duke
Mobley's shot, with 7 seconds left, propelled UK past No. 1 Duke, 81-79, in the Sugar Bowl. .

Kyle Macy
Feb. 24, 1980 vs. LSU
Macy's jumper gave the Cats the 1980 SEC crown, 76-74, in overtime.

Kenny Walker
Mar. 10, 1984 vs. Auburn
 The sophomore's 15-footer at the buzzer defeated Charles Barkley's squad for the SEC Tourney title.

Cedric Jenkins
Dec. 12, 1987 vs. Louisville
Jenkins' tip-in gave UK a 76-75 win against its arch rival.

Jeff Brassow
Dec. 23, 1993 vs. Arizona
Brassow tipped in a Rodrick Rhodes' miss as UK won the Maui Invitational, 93-92.

Walter McCarty
Feb. 15, 1994 vs. LSU
McCarty's three capped a 31-point comeback against the Tigers.

Tony Delk
April 1, 1996 vs. Syracuse
His three was part of a four-point play that lifted UK to its sixth NCAA title.

Scott Padgett
Mar.22, 1998 vs. Duke.
The three-pointer broke an 81-81 tie with 39.4 seconds left and capped a 17-point NCAA championship comeback.

Tayshaun Prince
Dec. 8, 2001 vs. North Carolina
This nearly 30' 3FG from just inside the mid-court logo capped five consecutive threes by Prince to open the game.

Patrick Sparks
Dec. 18, 2004 at Louisville
Sparks' three free-throws with no time remaining helped UK overcome a 16-point halftime deficit for a 60-58 win.

UK Athletics Hall of Fame Members

Member (Sport, Years)

Jeff Abbott (BB 1991-94)
Derek Abney (FB 2000-03)
George Adams (FB 1981-84)
Ermal Allen (FB 1939-41)
Sam Ball (FB 1963-65)
Cliff Barker (MBB 1947-49)
Ralph Beard (MBB 1946-49)
Calvin Bird (FB 1958-60)
Jerry Bird (MBB 1954-56)
Rodger Bird (FB 1963-65)
George Blanda (FB 1945-48)
Marsha Bond (VB 1980-83)
Sam Bowie (MBB 1980-81, '84)
Gay Brewer (MGolf 1952-54)
Pam Brauning (WB 1974-78)
AJ Bruno (FB 1948-50)
Paul "Bear" Bryant (FB Coach 1946-53)
Warren Bryant (FB 1974-76)
Bob Burrow (MBB 1955-56)
Burgess Carey (MBB 1925-26)
Mike Casey (MBB 1968-69, 71)
Jerry Claiborne (FB Coach 1982-89)
Blanton Collier (FB Coach 1954-61)
Sonny Collins (FB 1972-75)
Larry Conley (MBB 1964-66)
Ray Correll (FB 1951-53)
Tim Couch (FB 1996-98)
Johnny Cox (MBB 1957-59)
Louie Dampier (MBB 1965-67)
Bob Davis (FB 1935-37)
Dermontti Dawson (FB 1984-87)
Kathy DeBoer (VB 1984-02)
Tony Delk (MBB 1993-96)
John "Frenchy" DeMoisey (MBB 1932-34)
Leroy Edwards (MBB 1935)
Billy Evans (MBB 1952, '54-55)
Richie Farmer (MBB 1989-92)
Joe Federspiel (FB 1969-71)
Deron Feldhaus (MBB 1989-92)
Steve Flesch (MGOLF 1987-90)
Dom Fucci (BB 1948-51)
Bob Gain (FB 1947-50)
Jack Givens (MBB 1975-78)
Irv Goode (FB 1959-61)
Phil Grawemeyer (MBB 1954-56)
Jim Green (Track 1968-71)

Kevin Grevey (MBB 1973-75)
Alex Groza (MBB 1945, '47-49)
Wilbur Hackett (FB 1967-70)
Cliff Hagan (MBB 1951-52, '54)
Joe B. Hall (MBB Coach 1973-85)
Tim Harden (Track 1993-96)
Jenny Hansen (Gymnastics 1993-96)
Vernon Hatton (MBB 1956-58)
Basil Hayden (MBB 1920-22)
Mark Higgs (FB 1984-87)
J.B. Holmes (M Golf 2002-05)
Jim Host (Contributor/BB 1957-59)
Tom Hutchinson (FB 1960-62)
Dan Issel (MBB 1968-70)
Ilka Janttin (MSOC 1998-01)
Clyde Johnson (FB 1940-42)
Ellis Johnson (MBB, FB, Baseball, Track 1930-33)
Nancy Napolski Johnson (RIF 1993-96) .
Wah Wah Jones (MBB 1946-49, FB 1945-48)
Cedric Kaufmann (MTEN 1995-98)
Jeff Keener (BB 1980-81)
Bill Keightley (Equipment Mgr. 1962-2008)
John "Shipwreck" Kelly (FB 1929-31)
Ralph Kercheval (FB 1931-33)
Rick Kestner (FB 1963-65)
Rachel Komisarz (SW 1996-99)
Jim Kovach (FB 1974-76, '78)
Harry Lancaster (Director of Athletics,
   '968-75; Baseball Head Coach 1947, 1951-65;
   Assistant Men's Basketball Coach 1946-70)
Carwood Ledford (Broadcaster 1953-92)
Bill Lickert (MBB 1959-61)
Dicky Lyons (FB 1966-68)
Kyle Macy (MBB 1978-80)
Keith Madison (BB Coach 1979-2003)
Jamal Mashburn (MBB 1991-93)
Charlie McClendon (FB 1949-50)
Steve Meilinger (FB 1951-52-53)
Lou Michaels (FB 1955-56-57)
Doug Moseley (FB 1949-51)
Clayton Moss (Diving 1999-2003)
Colton Nash (MBB 1962-64)
C.M. Newton (MBB 1949-51; AD 1989-2000)
Rick Norton (FB 1963-65)
Rick Nuzum (FB 1972-74)
Johnny Owens (MGolf 1947-50)
Vito "Babe" Parilli (FB 1949-51)

John Pelphrey (MBB 1989-92)
Rick Pitino (MBB Coach 1990-97)
Mike Pratt (MBB 1968-70)
Tayshaun Prince (MBB 1999-02)
Derrick Ramsey (FB 1975-77)
Frank Ramsey (MBB 1951-52, '54)
Bill Ransdell (FB 1983-86)
Jay Rhodemyre (FB 1942, '46-47)
Russell Rice (SID 1967-87)
Pat Riley (MBB 1965-67)
Rick Robey (MBB 1975-78)
Dave Roller (FB 1968-70)
Kenny Rollins (MBB 1943, '47-48)
Gayle Rose (MBB 1952, '54-55)
Layton "Mickey" Rouse (MBB 1938-40)
Adolph Rupp (MBB Coach 1931-72)
Forest "Aggie" Sale (MBB 1931-33)
Howard Schnellenberger (FB 1952-55)
Nancy Scranton (W Golf 1983-84)
Larry Seiple (FB 1964-66)
Washington "Wash" Serini (FB 1944-47)
Bernie Shively (AD '38-67, FB Coach 1945)
Adrian Smith (MBB. 1956-58)
Carey Spicer (MBB 1929-31)
Bill Spivey (MBB 1950-51)
Art Still (FB 1974-77)
Valerie Still (WBB 1980-83)
Claude Sullivan (Sportscaster 1948-67)
Lou Tsioropoulos (MBB 1951-54)
Herschel Turner (FB 1961-63)
Harry Ullinski (FB 1946-49)
Jeff Van Note (FB 1966-68)
Kenny Walker (MBB 1983-86)
Brandon Webb (BB 1998-00)
Moe Williams FB (1993-95)
Sean Woods (MBB 1990-92)
Tina Johnson Ybarra (Diving 1994-96)
Craig Yeast (FB 1995-98)
Valerie McGovern Young (WXC 1988-91)

131

Chapter Seven
The Great Games

Although the University of Kentucky has played more than 2,500 basketball games since 1903, it is fairly easy to name the ones that stand out most in the hearts and minds of true UK fans. Surprisingly enough, the top five contains three games lost and two games won.

First and foremost is Duke's 104-103 overtime win over UK's "Untouchables" in the 1992 East Regional final at Philadelphia. The image of Duke's Christian Laettner's game-winning shot as time expired surely has set an all-time record for replays of a basketball moment.

Rick Pitino took to the City of Brotherly Love a team that featured sophomore Jamal Mashburn, and four seniors—Ritchie Farmer, Deron Feldhaus, John Pelphrey, and Sean Woods--who chose to remain loyal while others fled a UK program that was under NCAA probation.

That unlikely group clawed its way to 29 wins vs. seven losses before meeting defending national champion Duke, which was a prohibitive favorite. The two teams fought toe-to-toe until the final seconds of overtime, when Woods hit a 13-footer over Laettner to give UK a 103-102 lead with 2.1 seconds remaining.

During the timeout, Pitino chose not to guard the inbound man; instead, he told Feldhaus to front Laettner and Pelphrey to play in back of the Duke star. Grant Hill threw a liner to Laettner, who dribbled once, turned, and hit a 17-footer at the buzzer.

That was Laettner's 10th field goal in as many tries. He also hit all of his 10 free throw attempts to finish with 31 points. Mashburn led the Cats with 28 points.

Amidst Duke's celebration of the win over UK in the 1992 regional, Blue Devils coach Mike Krzyzewski walked over to Richie Farmer, put his arm around the UK guard, and said, "I'm sorry, Ritchie. I'm so sorry."

"What a tremendous, tremendous game," Coach K. told CBS. "It wasn't a game that anybody lost. Whoever had the ball last won. We beat a determined and great basketball team."

In retrospect, Pitino said that if he had it to do over again, he would station a man in front of Hill on the baseline. Since hindsight is 20/20, no one blamed him for the loss; in fact, they gloried in a fantastic season. The University hung jerseys of the "Unforgettables" in the rafters of Rupp Arena.

#2

Dayton, Ohio March 2, 1975
Kentucky 92, Indiana 90

Before the 1975 Mideast Regional game at Dayton, Joe B. Hall wrote on the blackboard: "NETS!" "BUS!" "POLICE!" "COLISEUM!" He wanted the players to be careful not to cut their fingers while cutting down the NETS; The BUS would be escorted by Kentucky State POLICE back to Lexington, where they would hold a victory celebration at the COLISEUM.

The Wildcats were heavy underdogs when they met Indiana. The Hoosiers were unbeaten in 34 games and rated No. 1. One of their victories was a 98-74 victory over UK earlier that season. During a sideline discussion with officials, IU's Bobby Knight cuffed UK's Coach Hall on back of the head.

Each team made 37 field goals, and each shot just under 50 percent from the field. They were tied, 44-44 at halftime. They continued to race along neck-to-neck until Rick Robey and Kevin Grevey put together eight straight points for the Wildcats.

Mike Phillips accounted for six points late in the game to give UK an 89-81 lead. When IU cut the lead to 92-90 with five seconds remaining, UK's Jimmy Dan Conner dribbled away the remaining time.

The Kentucky State Police, as promised, escorted the UK team bus and a long string of vehicles sporting blue and white banners, on the interstate. The overpasses and roadsides were

lined with cheering fans. A capacity crowd in the 11,500-seat
Memorial Coliseum welcomed home the conquering heroes.

#3

TEXAS WESTERN VS. UK
College Park, Md., March 19, 1966
Texas Western 72 Kentucky 65

*The Kentucky bench after loss to (#3) Texas Western, 65-72, in
1966 NCAA championship game in College Park, Md.*

Texas Western ranks third on the list for two reasons, one
sentimental, the other racial. It is a story of an all-white team
playing an integrated team that started five black players and
substituted only blacks that day.

The "lily-white" group called "Rupp's Runts"
represented a culture opposite that of the Miners, who mostly
were streetwise urbanites. The Wildcats had finished 15-10 the
preceding year and people were saying Rupp was getting too old,
letting the game pass him by.

As the team put together a string of 24 straight victories, they became the darlings of the basketball world and of Rupp, into whose barony they had breathed new life. Meanwhile, the Miners were an almost unknown entity, although they were rated No. 3, behind UK and Duke. The racial issue would not rear its ugly head until many years later, and mostly by persons who weren't familiar with the mood and circumstances of that era.

"Anyone who says that game wasn't all about race is in denial; it was about nothing but race," said William Turner, a leader of the Black Student Union at Kentucky in the mid-1960s and later a newspaper editorial writer in North Carolina.

Texas Western's all-black starting lineup featured Dave "Big Daddy D" Lattin, a 6-foot-7 smooth, agile, intimidating center who was perhaps the best unknown player in the country. Neville "The Shadow" Shed was a rugged forward and Harry Flournoy was an excellent rebounder. Bobby Joe Hill was only 5-foot-9, but his speed and quickness made up for a lack of size. Two other little men, Ortis Atis and "Wee" Willie Worsley, combined with Hill to give the Texans speed and outside shooting to cope with the Kentuckians.

The game turned midway of the first half when Hill stole the ball from Kron, dribbled half the length of the floor, and made a lay-up. Seconds later, Hill stole the ball from Louie Dampier and scored another uncontested lay-up. Kentucky got within two points in the second half, but lost, 72-65, to the Miners.

Riley called it the worst defeat of his life. "There was an unspoken feeling this was a significant game, even though it wasn't chronicled," he said. "It wasn't written about like it would be today."

#4

Baton Rouge, La., Feb. 15, 1994
Kentucky 99, LSU 95

135

The most dramatic comeback in UK basketball history and the second best in NCAA annals occurred on the night of Feb. 15, 1994, in Pete Maravich Assembly Center at Baton Rouge. Dale Brown's Tigers led Rick Pitino's Wildcats by 31 points (68-37) with 15:34 minutes to play, and fans back in the Bluegrass were turning off their radio and television sets.

The Tigers led, 48-32, at halftime and continued to pile it on until UK's outside shooters started hitting the mark. Led by the three-point shooting of Jeff Brassow, Walter McCarty and Chris Harrison, the Wildcats gradually fought their way back into contention. They took a 96-95 lead when McCarty hit a trey with 19 seconds remaining. LSU missed two chances to take the lead, and the Cats made three free throws to go home with an improbable 96-95 win.

Although Duke holds a record of coming from 32 down, the Blue Devils did it at home. Kentucky still holds the "away" record.

#5

San Diego, March 31, 1975
UCLA 92, Kentucky 85

When UCLA's legendary basketball coach John Wooden announced his retirement on the eve of the championship game of the 1975 NCAA Tournament, the Wildcat staff feared that would give the Bruins a psychological edge, which it did.

Kentucky led by five points at halftime, but Mike Phillips and Rick Robey got in foul trouble and the Wildcats were playing with what Coach Hall called his 13-13 squad of the previous year. The Bruins forged ahead by 70-61 with nine minutes to play, but the Wildcats cut it to 74-73. Dave Meyers hit two free throws to put UCLA ahead by a point; Kevin Grevey made a 20-footer with 6:45 remaining. Twenty seconds later, Meyer fouled Grevey and was assessed a technical foul for uttering a profanity. Both of Grevey's free throws rimmed out, but UK still retained possession. A Wildcat was called for an offensive pick on the baseline; a possible five points came up blank. UCLA built the lead to 82-77 and went on to win, 92-85.

Most Humiliating

Lexington, Jan. 8, 1955
Georgia Tech 59, UK 58

Fifty years after the fact, the biggest upset in UK Basketball history--Georgia Tech 59, UK 58--was just another entry in the record books. However, it was a monumental event when a mediocre Georgia Tech team ended the university's streak of 129 consecutive home wins in Alumni Gym and Memorial Coliseum.

Rupp told his players the night of January 8, 1955, would go down in infamy. "From this time until history is no longer recorded, you will be remembered as the team that broke the string," he said. "Even if you go on to win the NCAA championship, you must carry this scar with you the rest of your lives.

Lexington, March 16, 1960
Ohio State 82, Kentucky 81

The Wildcats had their bags packed, ready to travel for the Final Four in Los Angeles. The game boiled down to the final six seconds, when a missed shot by Ohio State was bobbled out of bounds by Mike Casey. Dave Sorenson took the ball on the throw-in and made a medium jump shot that gave OSU a one-point victory.

Capitalizing on Mistakes

Mental lapses by two foes—Kansas and Maryland— allowed UK to pull a victory from the jaws of defeat. They rank among UK's most unlikely wins.

Lexington, Dec. 15, 1958
Kentucky 58. Maryland 56 (OT)

The Terrapins were leading by three points with 15 seconds to play and UK in possession. During a timeout, Rupp said their only chance was for someone to drive for the basket, make it, and draw a foul. Maryland coach Bud Milliken told his players to let UK throw the ball in and score just don't commit a foul. The throw-in came to Bennie Coffman, who drove the lane, scored and was fouled by Al Bunge. Coffman made the free throw and a rejuvenated UK won in overtime.

Lexington, Dec. 9, 1978
Kentucky 57, Kansas 56

UK scored seven points in the final 31 seconds of overtime—the last three by junior guard Kyle Macy—to hand Kansas its first defeat in five games. The Wildcats trailed, 66-60 when an event that UK coach Joe B. Hall termed "amazing" occurred.

The sequence began when Dwight Anderson made two free throws that cut the Kansas lead to 66-64 with seconds remaining. Anderson then knocked the inbounds pass away from the Jayhawks' Mac Stallcup, saved the ball from going out of bounds, and slapped it all the way cross court to Macy. The Wildcat junior hit a 15-foot jump shot to tie the score with four seconds left.

Kansas star Darnell Valentine, apparently unaware that the rules allowed only one time-out in overtime, called for a break in action, which resulted in a technical foul with four seconds left. Macy sank the free throw that gave UK a one-point win.

Goodbye Games

When UK said goodbye to two arenas—Alumni Gym and Memorial Coliseum—that had been so good to them, victories in the final two games should have been no-brainers; however, Vanderbilt and Mississippi State thought otherwise.

Lexington, March 4, 1950
Kentucky 70, Vanderbilt 66

Trailing Vanderbilt at halftime, Rupp told his players, "Boys, a man spends a lifetime compiling a record, and in one night a bunch of bums like you are about to tear it down. If it looks like we're going to go down in defeat tonight, I want you to know that I am personally going to do something to this facility before the game is over and before you get out of this gym." UK's win that night preserved on ongoing record of 84 consecutive victories in the facility, where they had compiled a 262-25 record over the past 26 years.

Lexington, March 8, 1976
Kentucky 94, Mississippi State 93 (OT)

More than 12,000 fans gathered in overcrowded Memorial Coliseum to say goodbye to an arena that had been home of the Wildcats since 1950/51. During those 25 years, Kentucky teams had amassed 305 wins and 38 losses. They were favored to increase that win total against a Mississippi team that had compiled a 13-12 record up to that point.

State forged ahead by seven on three occasions, the last at 84-77 with only 1:23 to go. But UK fought back and tied the game with field goals by Larry Johnson and Jack Givens.

State took its only overtime lead at 87-85 on Wiley Peck's follow shot, but Givens—who led all scorers with 26 points along with nine rebounds and five assists—answered with a baseline jumper After Johnson and Peck traded baskets, Bob Fowler put UK ahead, 94-91. Ray White's last-second lay-up was too little and too late.

139

Rules-Changing Game

New York, Jan. 5, 1935
NYU 23, Kentucky 22

A foul goal by Sidney Gross in the last minute of play gave New York University a 23-22 triumph over UK in the feature game of a college double-header before basketball's largest crowd in Eastern court history. That record crowd of 16,500 witnessed a hammer-and-tong battle that was tied six times. It was a struggle between teams that exemplified two entirely distinct types of basketball.

The Violets displayed a brand of play that was indigenous to the East. It was one of the fast break, the quick-cut for the basket and a short flick-in. Kentucky on the other hand, employed a slow, deliberate style of offense that was built around 13 plays. The Wildcat also would fast break when an opportunity presented itself.

The score was never tied in the first half as UK led 9-8 at intermission. It was tied in the second at 9-all, 11-all, 13-all, 18-all, and then at 22-all. The pivot play between UK's LeRoy "Big Boy" Edwards and NYU's Irving "Slim" Tergensen and Roy "King Kong" Klein was so rough that it resulted in the Rules Committee widening the area around the basket.

What was called screening in the South was considered a blocking foul in the North. On the final displayed play, Edwards was accused of picking off Gross, who made the game-deciding free throw.

UK's Bill Spivey guards Clyde Lovellette during a 68-39 UK victory over the Jayhawks in December 1950, in Lexington. Spivey outscored the Kansas All American, 22-10.

Lexington, Dec. 16, 1950
Kentucky 68, Kansas 39

The "Battle of the Giants" turned into an embarrassment for Rupp's old Kansas Coach Phog Allen and Clyde Lovellette. The Wildcats were leading, 8-5, when they launched an assault that gave them a 20-6 cushion. They extended that to 68-39 as substitutes carried on in the last seven minutes. Spivey outscored Lovellette, 22-10.

Lexington, Nov 27, 1976

Kentucky 72, Kansas 64.

With Kansas native Adolph Rupp looking on, UK defeated the Jayhawks in the first game played in Rupp Arena. Robey had 13.Givens and Johnson each had 12.

Chapter Eight
The Twenty Best Teams

1) 1996 (34-2) NCAA – 1
2) 2012(38-2) NCAA - 1
3) 1948 (36-2) NCAA - 1
4) 1949 (32-2) NCAA – 1
5) 2010 (35-3) Final Four
6) 1978 (32-2) NCAA – 1
7) 1954 (25-0) Undefeated
8) 1951 (32-2) NCAA - 1
9) 1998 (35-4) NCAA - 1
10) 1952 (29-3) Elite Eight
11) 1970 (26-2) Region Final
12) 1997 (35-5) NCAA - 2
13) 1966 (27-2) NCAA -2
14) 1958 (23-6) NCAA – 1
15) 1992 (29-7) Region Final
16) 1947 (34-3) NIT - 2
17) 1984 (29-5) Final Four
18) 1986 (32-4) Elite Eight
19) 1993 (30-4) Final Four
20) 2003 (32-4) Region Final

1) 1995/96 (32-2): In choosing the 1995-96 Wildcats as the second best college basketball team of all time, ESPN said Rick Pitino's club was so good that they could have been a decent NBA team -- Antoine Walker, Tony Delk, Walter McCarty, Derek Anderson and Ron Mercer were first-round picks. Mark Pope was a second-round draft choice.

Even though the Wildcats lost two regular-season games (Massachusetts and Mississippi), they established themselves as one of the all-time great teams by destroying the competition in the "Big Dance," winning their six tourney games by an average of 21 points.

They were, by far, the deepest team in recent college basketball history, with so many stars that some were amazed that Pitino was able to keep it all together.

2) 2012 (38-2): John Calipari's team featured a lineup composed of three freshmen—Anthony Davis (14.2 ppg); Michael Kidd-Gilchrist (11.9); and Maquis Teague (10.0), and sophomores Doron Lamb (13.7) and Terrence Jones (12.3). Senior Darius Miller was the sixth man. That group played 40 games. They lost only to Indiana, 72-73, in Bloomington, and Vanderbilt, 64-71 in the SEC tournament.

Kentucky and Louisville met in the Final Four for the first time in history. Anthony Davis scored 18 points, grabbed 14 rebounds, and blocked five shots, leading the Cats to a 69-61 victory. They had also beat Louisville and Kansas, their next foe, earlier in the season.

Doron Lamb led all scorers with 22 points in a 67-59 win over the Jayhawks. Anthony Davis grabbed 16 rebounds, blocked six shots, and dished out five assists as UK won its eighth NCAA title.

Fabulous Five: Front, l to r, Ralph Beard, Coach Adolph Rupp, Kenny Rollins Back, Wallace Jones Alex Groza, Cliff Barker.

3) 1947/48 (36-3): The "Fabulous Five" lost only to Temple, 60-59, in Philadelphia, and to Notre Dame, 64-55, at South Bend. They swept the SEC and defeated Baylor, 77-59, in the NCAA championship game. Then they beat Louisville and Baylor again for the college trials championship. They lost to the Phillips Oilers, 49-53, for the Olympic Trials championship. The UK record for the most wins (36-3) in a season stood until 1986. They also set a record for average margin of victory, at 24.6 points, which still ranks as the tenth most ever.

Rupp called them the greatest team ever assembled in a college sport. Eyes filled with tears, he said, "You've done everything you've been asked to do. You won your own SEC tournament. You won the NCAA championship. You've kept training and made many sacrifices to do these things and for all of it I thank you from the bottom of my heart."

What the War initially took away from Rupp was generously returned in the Fall of 1947. Patton's Third Army freed Cliff Barker from a prisoner-of-war camp; a national ruling

145

allowed Ralph Beard and Wallace Jones to play four straight years together. The Army developed Alex Groza into the finest pivot man in the nation; and the Navy turned Kenny Rollins into a mature floor leader. This "Fabulous Five" was and still is considered one of the finest college basketball teams ever assembled.

Before the 1948 Olympic Trials, the U.S. Basketball Committee chose a 14-member Olympic squad that consisted of five members each from each team in the championship bracket and four from the other teams in each bracket. The coach of the winning team would be the head coach, with the coach of the second place team serving as associate coach.

After earning Gold Medals in the 1948 Olympics and repeating as NCAA champions in 1949, Barker, Beard, Groza, and Jones, joined by Joe Holland, formed the Indianapolis Olympians, an entry in the National Basketball Association. Beard and Groza starred two years on the team before a New York judge banned them from basketball for collegiate involvement with gamblers. The team disbanded the following year.

Kenny Rollins earned all-rookie honors with the Chicago Stags in 1949. He is a retired business executive (National Container Corp.) living in Florida. He died in 2013.

Barker spent three years as player-coach of the Indianapolis Olympians. He operated a restaurant in Frankfort before teaching and coaching basketball in Florida. Cliff died in 1988.

Beard retired as vice president for a wholesale drug company. An avid golfer, he played 18 holes a day, weather, and bad knees permitting. Ralph died in 2008.

Jones served a term as sheriff of Fayette County before entering the publishing business. He owns and operates Bluegrass Tours in Lexington.

Groza coached basketball at Bellarmine College and was an executive with the San Diego professional sports franchises. He was a vice president with Reynolds Aluminum Co. when he died in 1995.

4) 1948/1949 (32-2): Only Kenny Rollins did not return from Kentucky's 1948 "Fabulous Five" team. Dale Barnstable filled the vacancy. He joined a starting lineup that once again featured the All-American combination of Alex Groza and Ralph Beard, and forwards Wallace Jones and Cliff Barker. They won their sixth consecutive SEC title and were undefeated in league play for the third straight season.

The Fabulous Five Captain, Kenny Rollins, drives a nail to mark the spot in Alumni Gym where Ralph Beard made a 52.5 foot shot against Tennessee in 1948. Beard watches the ceremony, along with, left to right, standing, Rupp, Cliff Barker, Joe Holland, Alex Groza and Wallace Jones.

Kentucky and Oklahoma A&M played the NCAA championship game in Seattle. Rupp surprised Hank Iba by slowing the game down to A&M's pace. The Wildcats controlled the game so artistically that for one 12-minute stretch A&M failed to score a single field goal. Kentucky stalled for a 46-36 victory. Rupp had also entered the Wildcats in the NIT earlier that month, but Loyola of Chicago defeated the Cats, spoiling his bid to win both the big tournaments in one year.

In becoming the only team to win 30 or more games in three consecutive seasons, the Wildcats won 94.1 percent of their games, the best in school history.

5) 2010 (35-3): Kentucky featured three freshmen—John Wall 16), DeMarcus Cousins (15.1) and Eric Bledsoe (11.3)—a junior, Pat Patterson (14.3), and a sophomore, Darius Miller (6.5) as leading scorers on John Calipari's first team at UK. They won

148

both the SEC regular and tournament titles that year. They beat Cornell but lost to West Virginia in the East Regional. The freshmen turned pro.

Jack Givens goes up for two of his 41 points in UK's 94-88 win over Duke in the 1978 NCAA championship game in St. Louis.

6) 1977/78 (32-2): The "Twin Towers" of Rick Robey and Mike Phillips led a big and talented group of senior front court players that also included Jack Givens and James Lee. They were complemented well by sophomore guard Kyle Macy and his junior running mate Truman Claytor.

Kentucky began ranked number two in the polls, but spent the entire rest of the season, except two weeks, ranked number one. Their two losses were on the road to Alabama in January and LSU in February.

During the season, five Wildcats scored in double figures, including sixth man Lee. Macy set the school record for free throw accuracy, hitting 115 for 129 for 89.2 percent. Givens' 2,038 points were second only to Dan Issel (2,138) until Kenny Walker (2,080) moved into the runner-spot eight years later.

7) 1950/51 (32-2): Kentucky's impressive lineup featured seven-foot All-America center Bill Spivey, future All-Pro players, and Basketball Hall of Fame members Cliff Hagan and Frank Ramsey, and All-SEC forward Shelby Linville. The only senior on the roster was Walt Hirsch. Six Wildcats averaged more than nine points per game during the season. The only other NCAA champion to accomplish that feat was UCLA's 1995 team.

The Wildcats won their eighth straight SEC title, ranked third nationally in scoring (74.7 ppg) and first in scoring margin (24.3). They out-rebounded their 34 opponents 2,109-1,357. Spivey led the group with 567 boards, which still is a school record, followed by Ramsey (434) Shelby Linville (309), Hirsch (239), Cliff Hagan (169), and Lou Tsioropoulos (130).

That team gave Rupp and UK their third NCAA championship in four years, becoming the first school to capture three titles.

8) 1953/54 (25-0): From 1948-51, Kentucky won three national titles, and finished the 1952 season ranked number one before losing in the East Regional final. Because of the point-shaving scandals of the early-1950s, UK was forced to abort its entire 1953 schedule. When the Wildcats resumed play the following year, they posted a 25-0 record, but refused an invitation to the NCAA Tournament when it was ruled that post-graduate players Hagan, Ramsey and Tsioropoulos would be ineligible. LaSalle, the eventual champion, lost to Kentucky by 13 points earlier in the season.

1954 Team

9) 1998 (35-4): Tubby Smith won a national championship in his first season as head coach of the Wildcats. His team overcame double-digits three times in its march through the Big Dance. Duke led them by 17 points with 10 minutes to go in the South Regional. The Wildcats chipped away and emerged a winner by two points. They trailed Stanford by 10 in the second half, but the three-point shooting of Jeff Sheppard (27 points) helped UK to an 86-85 win. Down by 10 at halftime against Utah in the championship game, the Wildcats won, 78-69. It was the largest deficit ever overcome in a championship game

10) 1951-52 (29-3): Led by All-American Cliff Hagan, the 1952 Wildcats became the first team to average more than 80 points during a season. They finished atop the Associated Press and United Press polls, which were issued before the NCAA Tournament.

UK's season and 23-game winning streak ended when eventual runner-up St. John's defeated the Wildcats 64-57 in the East Regional final. Earlier in the season, Kentucky defeated St. John's by 41 points in Lexington.

Cliff Hagan virtually rewrote the conference book in scoring and was named to every major All-America team—in most instances the only junior on the first team. His high-scoring clutch performances were credited most of UK's success that season.

11) 1969/70 (26-2): When Mike Casey received a crushed leg in an automobile accident in the summer of 1969, Adolph Rupp said, "There goes our chance to win another NCAA." The Wildcat coach was probably right. During the past two years, the trio of Casey, Dan Issel, and Mike Pratt had compiled a 45-10 record and appeared in two NCAA tournaments.

Without Casey the 1970 team won 15 straight games before losing at Vanderbilt, 89-81. They won their remaining regular season games and defeated Notre Dame, 109-99, in the opening round of the Mideast Regional at Columbus, Ohio. They lost to Jacksonville, 100-106 in the regional final.

Dan Issel ended his career with a 28-point, 10-rebound performance that gave him career totals of 2,138 Points and 1.078 rebounds, school records that are still on the (men's) books.

12) 1996/97 (35-5): After losing such quality players as Tony Delk, Antoine Walker, Walter McCarty, and Mark Pope, Kentucky's chances of repeating as NCAA champions seemed slim. However, Rick Pitino reloaded and came out with a team that compiled a 35-5 record and advanced to the Final Four, losing an 84-79 thriller in overtime to Arizona in the championship game. Had Derek Anderson not gone down with a torn ligament midway of the season, the Wildcats conceivably could have gone all the way.

13) 1965/66 (27-2): All five "Rupp's Runts" averaged in double figures: Pat Riley, 21.9; Louie Dampier, 21.1; Thad Jaracz, 13.2; Larry Conley, 11.5, and Tom Kron, 10.2. They scored 90 percent of the team's total points and rebounds.

With sophomore center Thad Jaracz only 6-foot-5, the Wildcat team affectionately known as "Rupp's Runts." It was the smallest team ever to reach the Final Four, Louie Dampier and Pat Riley, both juniors, made -America, thanks to the unselfish play of seniors Larry Conley and Tom Kron. Dampier later became the all-time career scorer in the old American Football League. Riley played briefly with San Diego and Los Angeles. He became a pro Hall of Fame coach.

The Wildcats were 26-0 when they lost to Tennessee, 69-62, at Knoxville. They returned home and closed the season with a 103-74 win over Tulane. Although Texas Western was ranked third in the nation, they were heavy underdogs in a field that included No. 1 and No. 2 Duke. The NCAA semi-final game between the Wildcats and the Blue Devils was billed as the championship game. Kentucky defeated Duke, 83-79, but the game took a heavy toll on the tiring Wildcats. Meanwhile, Texas Western defeated Utah, 85-78, in the other semi and prepared a surprise for the Wildcats

Rupp and Johnny Cox

14) 1957-58 (23-6): The "Fiddlin' Five" won 19 of 25 games played in regular season. Never before had a team with six or more losses won an NCAA Tournament championship.

153

They played the Mideast Regional in Memorial Coliseum and the Final Four in Louisville's Freedom Hall. The Wildcats easily defeated Miami (Ohio) and Notre Dame in the regional, and edged Temple, 61-60, in a semi-final round of the Final Four. They defeated Seattle and the great Elgin Baylor, 84-72, in the championship game.

That The 1957/58 Wildcat basketball team mystified Rupp "They're fiddlers—be right entertaining at a barn dance", he said. "But I'll tell you, you need violinists to play at Carnegie Hall. We don't have any violinists."

Don Mills (54), A. B. "Happy" and Vernon Hatton celebrate UK's win over Seattle, 84-72, in the 1958 NCAA championship game in Seattle. Hatton led both teams in scoring with 30 points.

What Rupp had was a solid nucleus of four seniors—Ed Beck, John Crigler, Vern Hatton and Adrian Smith—backed by Johnnie Cox, the 1957 SEC sophomore of the year.

After winning All-America honors that year, Hatton spent four years with Philadelphia and St. Louis in the NBA. Smith played 10 years with Cincinnati in the NBA and one year in the

154

ABA. He was a member of the 1960 championship U. S. Olympic basketball team. Smith was Most Valuable Player in the 1966 NBA All-Star Game. Cox also won All-America honors in 1959, played semi-pro ball before spending one year in the NBA.

In presenting UK its fourth NCAA championship, the "Fiddlers" outscored their opponents, 2,166-1,817. They put no new entries in the UK record book. However, Rupp pointed to the scoreboard and said, "These boys are not concert violinists, but they certainly can fiddle".

"Unforgettables"

15) 1991-92 (29-7): Dubbed the "Unforgettables" because it consisted mostly of players who chose to remain throughout a period of probation, the 1992 UK team won both the SEC season and tournament championships and advanced to the ""Elite Eight." Their overtime 104-103 loss to Duke is considered one of the finest basketball game ever played. UK inducted the five starters—Jamal Mashburn (21.3), John Pelphrey (12.5), Deron Feldhaus (11.4), Richie Farmer (9.6), and Sean Woods (7.7 into its athletic HOF.

16) 1946-47 (34-3): Five native Kentuckians—Ralph Beard, Joe Holland, Jack Tingle, Kenny Rollins and Wallace

Jones—made first-team All-SEC. They outscored their opponents by an average of 30 points, but lost to Utah, 49-45, in the NIT.

17) 1983-84 (29-5): Despite a loss to Georgetown in the Final Four, the Wildcats had their best season since 1978. They won the SEC season and tournament titles and finished No. 3 in both wire service polls.

18) 1985-86 (32-4): In his debut as UK coach, Eddie Sutton leads the Wildcats to the Elite Eight, where they lost, 59-57, to an LSU team they defeated on three previous outings that season.

19) 1992-93 (30-4): The Wildcats lose to Michigan in overtime in the NCAA semi-finals. Travis Ford sets a UK season record with 101 three-point field goals.

20) 2002-03 (32-4): Kentucky sweeps the SEC (16-0) and wins the conference tournament; but the run ends with an 83-69 loss to Marquette in the Midwest Regional.

Chapter Nine
The Most All-Around Players

Multi-Sports Performers

1, Wallace Jones (1946-49)—"Wah Wah" earned four letters each in basketball and football, and three in baseball. He was All-America, basketball, All-SEC football.

2. Ellis Johnson (1931-32-33)—Ellis won three letters each in baseball, basketball, and football. He also lettered in track.

3. Cotton Nash (1962-64)—Cotton was All-America in basketball and a star pitcher/first baseman at UK. He won the SEC freshman discus event in 1961 and finished fifth in the 1963 SEC track meet. Nash is one of only a handful of athletes to play both NBA basketball and Major League baseball.

4. Charles Hughes (1924-25)—"Turkey" lettered in baseball, basketball, football, and track at UK.

5. Carey Spicer (1929-31)—Carey was a two-time All-America and team captain in basketball, a football quarterback, and a tennis letterman.

Strongest

1-LeRoy Edwards (1935)—How strong was "Big Boy?" Rupp said Edwards could break the cable on the Golden Gate Bridge.

2-Mike Pratt (1968-70)—A rugged enforcer on three SEC championship teams.

3-Charles Hurt (1980-83)—Cawood Ledford called him "Tarzan".

4-Marcus Cousins (2010)—At 6-foot-11, nobody crossed Cousins.

5-Dan Issel (1968-70)—They didn't call him "Hoss" for nothing.

6-Pat Riley (1965-67)—Rupp said Riley was one of the strongest athletes he ever coached.

RILEY HIGH SCHOOL

Pat Riley averaged 29.5 points and hit the 1,000-mark during his senior season at Linton High School in Schenectady, N. Y. He scored more than 40 points in each of the final four games. Riley also gained All-America recognition as a football quarterback. When Rupp heard that Riley had visited Bear Bryant at Alabama and Joe Paterno at Penn State, the Baron scheduled the next flight to New York.

Riley became familiar with the UK program through the great UK teams that visited New York and the East. He confided to Rupp that as a kid he wanted to come to Kentucky. "It was almost like my future was predetermined," he said. "I was going to play basketball. When Adolph flew in, that sealed it."

Pure Shooters

1. Louie Dampier (1965-67)—Louie compiled a 50.8 career field goal percentage at UK, mostly from medium and long range. His 19.7 scoring average is tops among UK guards. Dampier was the all-time scoring leader in the ABA.

2. Charles Hurt (1980-83)—Playing a forward, Hurt's main role was not as a shooter, but he shot an impressive 59.3 percent (303 of 511) to lead the career percentage list.

3. Kyle Macy (1978-80)--Macy made 52.1 percent of his field goal attempts. He holds the school record (89.0 %) for free throw percentage. Kyle played seven pro seasons, hitting more than 50 percent of his field goal attempts.

4. Vernon Hatton—Vern is the only guard to lead the Cats in field goal percentage three years in a row.

5. Derrick Miller—Derrick's performance in the 1998 Great Alaska Shootout proved that Rick Pitino had inherited one fine shooter from the remnants of NCAA sanctions.
(Freshman Myron Anthony hit 67.4% (9-144) and 76.6% of his free throws in 1998; Sophomore Terrence Jones made 83-149 for 55.7 %.in 2012)

Assists

1. Cliff Barker (1947-49)—The war veteran was known as the "Houdini of the Hoops", for the magic he developed playing with volleyballs in a German POW camp.

2. Dirk Minniefield (1980-83)—Dirk is UK's all-time leader in career assists (646).

3. Roger Harden—The Indiana native loved to throw "Oop" passes to Sam Bowie.

4. Sean Woods—This "Untouchable" is UK's all-time assists-per-game leader with 5.53 apg in 91 games.

159

5. Larry Conley (1964-66)—"Rupp's Runts" passing wizard was the first Wildcat to lead the team in assists two consecutive years.

Rebounders

1-Bill Spivey (1950-51)—The 7-footer pulled down 34 boards against Xavier in 1951. His season total of 567 that year still is the UK season leader. If they had recorded rebounds prior to 1951 and Spivey had played his senior season, he undoubtedly would reign as UK's all-time rebounder.

2-Bob Burrow (1955-56)—Bob was a junior college transfer who tied Spivey with 34 boards against Temple. His 16.1 rpg average tops the UK list.

3-Cliff Hagan (1951-52, 54)—At 6-foot-4, the "Cat" possessed great timing. He is second to Burrow with a 13.4 career average.

4-Dan Issel (1968-70)—"Hoss" heads the career list with 1,078 rebounds in three seasons.

5-Cotton Nash (1962-64)—Cotton pulled down 30 boards against Temple in 1961/62 and Ole Miss. in 1963/64.

6-Anthony Davis (2012)--Anthony only played one year at UK, but he made his presence on the boards with 415 in 40 games.

3-Point Shooters

1-Travis Ford (1992-94)—This deadeye hit 52.9 percent (101/191) of his treys, which leads the UK list.

2-Tony Delk (1993-96)—Tony is UK's career leader with 283 treys. His 9 of 12 vs. TCU is a single game high. Tony owns a record streak of 34 consecutive games with 3-point field goal.

3-Jodie Meeks ((2009)—Jodie made 10 treys in 15 attempts against Tennessee in Knoxville. He made nine treys in three other games that season.

4-Derrick Miller (1987-90)—Derrick knocked down seven treys and scored 36 points in an 89-71 win over California in the Great Alaska Shootout. He was a bright spot in a 13-19 season, Pitino's first at UK.

5-Jamal Mashburn (1991-93)—"Monster Mash" could step out of the paint and hit the treys. He made 43.9 percent of his shots from beyond the arc.

Sixth Man

Darius Miller

Darius Miller (2012)—Darius played in all 40 games while earning 11 starts his senior year. ... He averaged 9.9 points and made 56 3-pointers

Kyle Wiltjer

Kyle Wiltjer (2013)--Wiltjer averaged 10.2 points and 4.2 rebounds per game in 33 games, including 10 starts, as a sophomore. The SEC chose him as Sixth Man of the Year.

Ron Mercer (1996)—Mercer came off the bench and scored 20 vital point in UK's 76-67 win over Syracuse in the

1996 NCAA championship game. After scoring 288 points as a reserve, Mercer, scored 725 points the following year. His two-year total of 1013 points ranks him No. 55 among all-time UK scorers.

James Lee (1974-78)—Lee scored 996 points **in** four years for the Wildcats, mostly in a reserve role. The Associated press named him third team All-SEC. Lee was a sometime starter who was fourth-leading scorer on UK's 1978 M\NCAA championship team.

Underappreciated

Ed Davender (1985-88) —"Ed Davender is arguably the most underappreciated guard in UK history. He ended his career with 1,637 points, 436 assists and 191 steals."...Tom Wallace.

Adrian Smith (1956-58)—"Odie" played 11 years in the pro's, was MVP of the 1966 NBA all-star game, and winner of an Olympic Gold Medal.

Reggie Hanson (1988-91)—Scoring leader of the "Untouchables", finished career with 1,167 points, 545 rebounds.

Saul Smith (1998-01)--It's tough playing when your father is the coach.

Sean Sutton (1988-89)—Ditto.

Shot Blockers

Anthony Davis

Anthony Davis (2012)—Anthony was the 2011–12 NCAA Division I men's basketball season blocks leader with 4.7 bpg. He established Southeastern Conference single-season blocked shots and NCAA Division I freshman blocked shots records

Sam Bowie (1980-81, '84)—The big guy blocked 218 shots in 96 games for a 2.271 average, which leads that category.

Jamal Maglioire

Jamal Maglioire (1997-00)—Jamal blocked more shots (268) than Bowie, but he also played in 51 more games; still, his per game average of 1,848 is third in the UK record book.

Melvin Turpin (1981-84)—Mel teamed with Sam Bowie for an awesome twosome around the basket. He blocked 226 shots in 123 games for a 1.837 average

Andre Riddick (1982-85)—Andre led the Wildcats in blocks each of his four years at UK. He and Melvin Turpin are tied for most blocks in a season with 83 each.

Bill Spivey (1950-51)—It's unfortunate that blocked shots were not recognized stats in Spivey's first varsity year at UK; otherwise, he might be leading the list.

Steals

Rajon Rondo (2005-2006)—Rondo leads the Cats in steals per game (2.29), and steals per season (87). He had 136 steals in two years at UK.

Wayne Turner holds the record at 151 for most games played.

Wayne Turner (1996-99)—With 238 steals, Turner leads UK's career list. His 79 thefts in 1996-97 were tops for the Cats that season, so were eight steals against George Washington the following year.

Derek Anderson

Derek Anderson (1996-97). An injury in mid-season cut short Derek's career, but he averaged 1.782 steals in 55 games to take UK career honors in that category.

Tony Delk (1993-96)—The long arms of Delk resulted in 201 steals, second only to Wayne Turner. He led the team his junior and senior years.

Cliff Hawkins (2001-04)—Hawkins registered 199 steals in 125 games for a 1.6 average, which is third on UK's list.

5. Ed Davender (1985-88)—This versatile defender is credited with 191 steals in 129 games (1.5). He led the team two years.

Best Free-Throw Shooters

Kyle Macy (1978-80)—Macy's free-throw shooting saved the Cats in many tight situations. He hit a UK school career record 89.0 percent 331/372) of his attempts. Kyle made 32 consecutive free throws from1979 to 1980.

Jodie Meeks

Jodie Meeks (2007-0009)—Jodie made 299 of 336 (89.0%) free throws, tying Kyle Macy's school record during three years at UK.

Travis Ford (1993-94)—This pure shooter made 88.2 percent of his freebees, only 00.8% off the school mark. Travis made 50 consecutive free throws (1992/93-1993-94) to lead in that category.

Jim Master (1981-84)—Another eagle eye (84.2%) who hit 95 of 106 (89.6%) his sophomore year. Master made 40 consecutive freebees in 1981/82.

Kenny Walker (1983-86)—This versatile All-American leads the Wildcats in career free-throws attempted (733) and made (550).

Dan Issel (1968-70)--With 488 made in 661 attempts, Dan ranks second to Walker in career free throws made (488) and attempted (661): however, Kenny played in 49 more games than Dan.

Best Dunkers

1-Kenny Walker—After thrilling Wildcat fans for four years, "Sky" won an NBA slam-dunk contest while with the New York Knicks.

2-James Lee—His thundering dunk to put the exclamation mark on UK's championship win over Duke in 1978 was one of many for the big southpaw.

3-Rex Chapman—Who said white men can't jump?

4-Walter McCarty—His dunks lit up his face, and the crowd.

5-Dirk Minniefield—As a guard, Dirk held his own with the aircraft carriers.

Retired Jerseys

Basil Hayden (1920-21-22), Burgess Carey (1925-26), Carey Spicer (1929-30-31), Adolph Rupp (1931-72), Forest "Aggie" Sale (1931-32-33), John "Frenchy" DeMoisey (1932-33-34), Layton "Mickey" Rouse (1938-39-40), Kenny Rollins (1946-47-48), Alex Groza (1945-47-48-49), Ralph Beard (1946-47-48-49), Wallace Jones (1946-47-48-49), Cliff Barker (1947-48-49), Bill Spivey (1950-51), Frank Ramsey (1951-52-54), Cliff Hagan (1951-52-54), Lou Tsioropoulos (1951-52-54), Billy Evans (1953-54-55), Gayle Rose (1952-54-55), Cawood Ledford (1953-92), Jerry Bird (1954-55-56) Phil Grawemeyer (1954-55-

56), Bob Burrow (1955-56), Vernon Hatton (1956-57-58), Johnny Cox (1957-58-59), Bill Keightley (1962-Present), Cotton Nash (1962-63-64), Louie Dampier (1965-66-67), Pat Riley (1965-66-67), Dan Issel (1968-69-70), Joe B. Hall (Head Coach--1973-85), Kevin Grevey (1973-74-75), Jack Givens (1975-76-77-78), Rick Robey (1975-76-77-78), Kyle Macy (1978-79-80), Sam Bowie (1980, 81, 84), Kenny Walker (1983-84-85-86), Richie Farmer (1989-90-91-1920), Deron Feldhaus (1989-90-91-92), John Pelphrey (1989-90-91-92), Sean Woods (1990-91-92), Jamal Mashburn ((1`991-92-93), Rick Pitino (Head Coach—1990-97).

Most Dedicated Fans

1. A. B. Chandler—"Happy" once coached the UK women's basketball team. The former Kentucky governor, senator, and baseball commissioner was UK's most ardent supporter until his death. He was a close friend of Adolph Rupp He came to the baron's defense during the gambling scandals of the '50's. Happy often sang "My Old Kentucky Home" before UK basketball games.

2. Steve Rardin—The Lexington magazine distributor with the Kentucky Colonel goatee missed UK's 1968 New Year's Eve loss to Wisconsin in Chicago due to a family wedding. He started a new "streak", which totaled 627 consecutive games before he suffered a heart attack while attending a road game at Syracuse in 1986. Steve died three years later.

3. Bob Wiggins—A traveling companion of Steve Rardin, Wiggins took up the attendance banner and attended 615 consecutive games before also suffering a heart attack on a trip to the Great Alaska Shootout in 1996. Wiggins has attended more than 1,500 UK games, at home and on the road.

4. Ashley Judd-- Anyone who watches UK games on TV knows exactly how this popular actress feels about her alma mater's basketball teams. Ashley even penned an article for Sports Illustrated that lauded the Wildcat program.

Actress Ashley Judd is an eighth generation Eastern Kentuckian who graduated from UK in 1990 with honors (Phi Beta Kappa.) she proudly wears and swears by the Blue & White.

Ashley was in her sixth month starring as Maggie in Cat on a Hot Tin Roof on Broadway when she injured her left foot in a performance in February 2004. Her first thought was that she could catch the remaining games on UK's schedule. She flew to Lexington in early March to watch the Cats beat South Carolina, 84-65.

It is customary during the first timeout of the second half for UK cheerleaders to spell out KENTUCKY and ask a person from the crowd to come out and make the Y.

One of Ashley's fondest memories occurred during "Senior Day" that month when cheerleader Jason Keogh shoulder-carried her (and the blue-painted cast on her left foot) to mid-court," "Before I was even introduced, I was given a standing ovation." she said. "It was the most extraordinary feeling."

"One thing I love about going to UK games is that I don't feel like a movie star," she said. "I'm just another passionate fan."

Ashley Judd

5. (tie) Bill Keightley—"Mr. Wildcat" was associated with the UK basketball equipment room for almost a half-century His love of the Cats was stronger than the strongest...etc. He traced his allegiance to the old Kavanaugh Prep School at Lawrenceburg, which produced such well-known Wildcats as Aggie Sale, Paul McBrayer, and Ralph Carlisle.

Oscar Combs—After selling The Cats' Pause, Oscar purchased a winter home in Florida, but that was too far from his beloved Wildcats. Oscar has a radio program in Lexington.

Wildcats in the Basketball Hall of Fame
Enshrined in Springfield, Mass.

Adolph Rupp
Inducted 1969

Cliff Hagan
Inducted 1978

Frank Ramsey
Inducted 1982

Dan Issel
Inducted 1993

C.M. Newton
Inducted 2000

Pat Riley
Inducted 2008

Adrian Smith
Inducted 2010

Joe B. Hall
Inducted 2012

173

Wildcat Lettermen

A

Allan Abramson, Mgr. ('44)
John Adams (63, 64,), 65)
Don Adkins (1963 64, 65)
Earl Adkins (1955, 57, 58)
Paul Adkins (1921, 22)
Marvin Akers 41, 42, 43)
Charles Alberts (1925, 26)
Charles Aleksinas (1978)
Ermal Allen (1940, 41, 42)
S. Alleyne (2004, 05, 06)
Ed Allin (1945)
D. Allison (1999, 00)
Sean Alteri (Mgr.) (1997)
Carl Althaus (1943)
H, M, Amoss (1904)
Derek Anderson (1996, 97)
Dwight Anderson (1979)
M.illerd Anderson (1934,-36)
Jim Andrews (1971, 72, 73)
Paul Andreus (1984-87)
Lee Andrus (1902, 04
Myron Anthony (1998)
 Phil Argento (1967, 68,69,)
R. H, Arnett (1904)
Jay Atkerson (Mgr.) (1957-59),
Randy Azbill (M) (1984, 85)
K. Azubuike (2003, 04, 05)

B

HA Babb (M) (1911)
Adrian Back (1942)
Stanley Baer (1905-07),
Scotty Baesler (1962, 63)
Mike Ballenger (1982)
RC, Barbee (1906-07, 09)
Anthwan Barbour (03, 04)
Cliff Barker (1947, 48, 49)
Bill Barlow (1943)
B, Barnett (1911, 12, 13)
Dale Barnstable (1947, 48, 49) 50)
Bobby Barton (Mgr.) (1967)
Will Barton Mgr.) 2010, 11)
Arthur Bastin (1918)

174

Dickey Beal (1981, 82, 83, 84)
Ralph Beard (1946-49)
Bret Bearup (1981 83, 84, 85)
Todd Bearup (1991)
Ed Beck (1956, 57, 58)
Cecil Bell (1931)
Winston Bennett (1984, 85, 86, 88)
Cliff Berger (1966, 67, 68)
Henry Besuden (1926)
Bill Bibb (1954)
Arthur Bicknell (1940)
Doug Billips (Mgr.) (1969, 70)
Jerry Bird (1954, 55, 56)
James Blackmon (1984, 85, 86, 87)
Crittenden Blair (1934)
Eric Bledsoe (2010)
J.P. Blevins (1999, 2000, 01, 02)
Harry Bliss (1935)
Keith Bogans (2000, 01, 02, 03)
J, David Bolen (Mgr.) (1996, 97, 98)
Ralph Boren (1924)
Brad Bounds (1966, 67)
Sam Bowie (1980, 81, 84)
Junior Braddy (1990, 91, 92, 93)
Michael Bradley (1998, 99)
Ramel Bradley (2005, 06, 07, 08)
Bob Brannum (1944, 47)
Jeff Brassow (1990, 91, 93, 94)
D, P' Branson (1905, 06)
Wayne Breeden (Mgr.) (1983)
John Brewer (1955, 56, 57)
Leo Brewer (1908)
Melvin Brewer (1941, 42, 43)
G, C, Bridges (1910)
Chris Briggs (Mgr.) (2002, 03, 04)
Jake Bronston (1930, 31)
Dale Brown (1992, 93)
Steve Bruce (1987)
T.R Bryant (1905, 06, 07)
Nathanial Buis (1944)
Carey Burchett (Mgr.) (1934)
Carroll Burchett (1960, 61, 62))
 LS, Burhham (1919, 20, 22, 23)
Bob Burrow (1955, 56)
Bill Busey (1968)
Kirk Byars (Mgr.) (1963)
Leroy Byrd (1984, 85, 86)

C

Craig Callihan (Mgr.) (2008, 09, 10)
Gerry Calvert (1955, 56, 57)
Jules Camara (1999, 2000, 02, 03)
George Campbell (Mgr.) (1935)
Kenton Campbell (1945, 46)
Patrick Campbell (1917, 18)
Will Campbell (Mg-2007-2010))
Burgess Carey (1925, 26)
Ralph Carlisle (1935, 36, 37)
Armiel Carman (Mgr.) (1916)
Josh Carrier (2002, 03, 04, 05)
Rashaad Carruth (2002)
Jared Carter (2006, 07, 08, 09)
Dwane Casey (1976, 77, 78, 79)
Mike Casey (1968, 69, 71)
Billy Ray Cassady (1956, 57, 58)
J, S, Chambers (Mgr.) (1909)
Rex Chapman (1987, 88)
Truman Claytor (1976, 77, 78, 79)
Steve Clevenger (1966, 67, 68)
Marion Cluggish (1938, 39, 40)
Bennie Coffman (1959, 60)
Sid Cohen (1959, 60)
L, Collinsworth (1956, 57, 58)
Carl Combs (1940)
Cecil Combs (1928, 29, 30)
Charles Combs (1938)
Larry Conley (1964, 65, 66)
Jimmy Dan Conner (1973, 74, 75)
Joe Coons (1905)
Anthony Cooper (1990)
Bernard Cote (2003, 04)
Mark Coury (2007, 08)
DeMarcus Cousins (2010)
Fred Cowan (1978, 79, 80, 81)
Jeremiah Cox (Mgr.) (2004, 05, 06)
Johnny Cox (1957, 58, 59)
Hugh Coy (1954)
Joe Crawford (2005, 06, 07, 08)
John Crigler (1956, 57, 58)
George Critz (1964)
Larry Crosby (Mgr.) (1965)
John S, Crosthwaite (1910)
Albert Cummins (1947)
Fred Curtis (1937, 38, 39)

D

Louie Dampier (1965, 66, 67)
Erik Daniels (2001, 02, 03, 04)
Darrell Darby (1931, 32, 33)
Howard Dardeen (1959)
Ed Davender (1985, 86, 87, 88)
A J. Davis (Mgr.) (2006)
Berkley Davis (1934)
Bruce Davis (1936)
Johnathon Davis (1989, 90, 91)
Mulord Davis (1943, 46, 47)
Robert Davis (1937)
William Davis (1933, 34)
David Deaton (Mgr.) (1989)
Ted Deeken (1962, 63, 64)
Claire Dees (1927, 28, 29)
Tony Delk (1993, 94, 95, 96)
John "Frenchy" DeMoisey 1932-34))
Truitt DeMoisey (1944)
Harry Denham (1939)1939) (1939
Rodney Dent (1993,, 94)
Jim Dinwiddie (1969, 70, 71)
J.A. Dishman (1918, 19)
Darnell Dodson (2010)
A. L. Dolan (1906)
Mike Dolan (Mgr.) (1952, 54)
Warfield Donohue (1935-37)
H.H. Downing (08)
Pat Doyle (1963)
RickDrewitz1972, 73, 74)
HunterDurham (M) (1961-, 62) J
James Durham (1945)

E

Ray Edelman (1972, 73, 74)
Allen Edwards (1995, 98)
Leroy Edwards (1935)
Russell Ellington1935, 36,
 LeRon Ellis (1988, 89)
Randy Embry (1963, 64, 65)
Kenneth England (1941, 42)
Anthony Epps (1994 -97)
Marquis Estill (2001, 02, 03)
Bill Evans (1952, 54, 55)
HeshimuEvans (1998, 99)
Mark Evans (M (2010, 11, 12))
William Evans (Mgr. (1942)
J.C. Everett (1919, 20)

F

H.L. Farmer (1912, 13)
Richie Farmer (1989, 90, 91, 92)
Keith Farnsely (1939, 40, 41)
John Farris (Mgr.) (1992, 94, 95)
J.B. Faulconer (Mgr.) (1939)
Allen Feldhaus (1960, 61, 62)
Deron Feldhaus (1989-92)
John Ferguson (Mgr.) (1971)
Fred Fest (1923)
Gerald Fitch (2001, 02, 03, 04)
Garrett Fitzpatrick (Mgr.) (1941)
George Fletcher (Mgr.) (1980, 81)
Chigger Flynn (Mgr.) (1956)
Mike Flynn (1973, 74, 75)
Bob Fowler (1976)
Travis Ford (1992, 93, 94)
WC. Fox (1907, 08, 09)
Jeremy French (Mgr.) (2007, 08, 09)

G

J.H. Gaiser (1910, 11, 12)
Kevin Galloway (2009)
Gary Gamble (1966, 67, 68)
Kenneth Gayheart (Mgr.) (1990, 91, 92, 94)
Robert Gayheart (Mgr.) (1989)
OJ. Geddes (Mgr.) (2001-05)
Chris Gettelfinger (1980, 81)
Elmer Gilb (1929)
Jeff Ginnan (1989)
Jack Givens (1975, 76, 77, 78)
Max Glickman (1918)
James Goforth (1935, 36, 37)
Zach Goines (Mgr.) (1996, 97, 98, 99)
James Goodman (1938, 39)
Steve Goodson (Mgr.) (2002-05)
Archie Goodman (2013)
Phil Grawemeyer (1954, 55, 56)
Sean Gray (Mgr.) (1994, 95, 96, 97)
Kevin Grevey (1973, 74, 75)
William Griffeth (Mgr.) (1929)
Alex Groza (1945, 47, 48, 49)
George Gumbert (1914, 15, 16)
Bob Guyette (1973, 74, 75)
J. White Guyn (1904)

H

Cliff Hagan (1951, 52, 54)
Joseph Hagan (1936, 37, 38)
Jerry Hale (1973, 74, 75)
Dan Hall (1975)
Mark Halsell (2009)
Reggie Hanson (1988, 89, 90, 91)
Roger Harden (1983, 84, 85, 86)
Philip Haring (Mgr.) (1936, 38)
Sam Harper (1963, 64)
Tom Harper (1964)
Carson Harreld (Mgr.) (1965, 66)
Josh Harrellson (2009, 10, 11)
Ramon Harris (2007, 08, 09, 10)
Chris Harrison (92, 93, 94, 95)
WC. Harrison (1911, 12)
D.W Hart (1911, 12, 16)
Merion Haskins (1975, 76, 77)
Vernon Hatton (1956, 57, 58)
Cliff Hawkins (2001, 02, 03, 04)
Basil Hayden (1920, 21, 22)
Chuck Hayes (2002, 03, 04, 05)
Elmo Head (1937, 38, 39)
Matt Heissenbuttel (2001, 02, 03, 04)
Tom Heitz (1980, 82, 83, 84)
G. Foster Helm (1925, 27)
J.H. Herman (1906)
Will Herschelman (Mgr.) (2006, 07, 08,
Walter Hirsch (1949, 50, 51) Walter Hodge (1937)
Ryan Hogan (1998, 99)
Joe Holland (1946, 47, 48)
Joey Holland (1976)
Kent Hollenbeck (1970, 71, 72)
Jon Hood (2010, 11, 13)
Derrick Hord (1980, 81, 82, 83)
Aaron Howard) Mgr.) 1998, 02)
Mike Howard (Mgr.) (1996, 97, 98:
Dick Howe (1957, 58)
 Lee Huber (1939, 40, 41)
C.T Hughes (1924, 25)
Lowell Hughes (1958, 59)
Harry Hurd (1962)
Charles Hurt (1980, 81, 82, 83)

I

R.Y.lreland (1916, 17)
Charles Ishmael (1963, 64)
Dan Issel (1968, 69, 70)

J

Ralph Jackowski (1938)
Thad Jaracz (1966, 67, 68)
Derrick Jasper (2007, 08)
Irvine Jeffries (1928)
Cedric Jenkins (1985, 86, 87, 88)
Paul Jenkins (1926, 27, 28)
Ned Jennings (1959, 60, 61)
Herbert Jerome (1934)
Danny Jett (Mgr.) (2003)
Ellis Johnson (1931, 32, 33)
Larry Johnson (1974, 75, 76, 77)
Phil Johnson (1956, 58, 59)
Walter Johnson (1944)
Chris Jones (1989)
Terrence Jones (2011, 12)
Wallace Jones (1946, 47, 48, 49)
James Jordan (1947, 48)
David Judy (Mgr.) (2000, 01 02)

K

Pat Kelly (1905)
William R Kemper (Mgr.) (1905)
Ron Kennett (1964)
Stan Key (1970, 71, 72)
Jeff Kidder (Mgr.) (1989)
James King (1940, 41, 42)
W William King (1921, 22, 24)
A.M. Kirby (1907)
William Kleiser (1932)

L

Art Laib (1968)
Doron Lamb (2011)
Ed Lander (1942, 43)
Bo Lanter (1980, 81, 82)
Jason Lathrem (1996)
Bob Lavin (1920, 21, 22)
Dave Lawrence (1933, 34, 35)
Roger Layne (1951)
James Lee (1975, 76, 77, 78)
Ken Lehkamp (Mgr.) (1956, 57)
Jim LeMaster (1966, 67, 68)
Preston LeMaster (2003, 04, 05, 06)
Larry Lentz (1966)

Morris Levin (Mgr.) (1931)
Garland Lewis (1934, 35, 36)
Billy Ray Lickert (1959, 60, 61)
DeAndre Liggins (2009, 10, 11)
James Line (1947, 48, 49, 50)
Shelby Linville (1950, 51, 52)
Zach Lipson (Mgr.) (2011)
Ercel Little (1932)
Steve Lochmueller (1973, 74)
Robert Lock (1985, 86, 87,
Brian Long (2012)
Dutch Longworth (1917)
Ronnie Lyons (1972, 73, 74)

M

Kyle Macy (1978, 79, 80)
Riphard Madison (1985, 86, 87, 88)
Jamaal Magloire (1997, 98, 99, 00)
Eric Manuel (1988)
Dustin Marr (Mgr.) (2006, 07, 08)
B.G. Marsh (1918)
Will Martin (Mgr.) (2009, 10, 11)
Gimel Martinez (1991, 92, 93, 94)
Sam Malone (2012, 13)
F.L. Marx (1910, 11)
Jamal Mashburn (1991, 92, 93)
Steve Masiello (1997-, 2000)
Luke Mason (Mgr.) (2007, 08)
Jim Master (1981-84,)
James Mathewson (1942)
Charles Maxson (Mgr.) (1933)
Jack May (Mgr.) (1935, 36)
Julius Maya) 2013)
John McAdam (Mgr.) (1970)
Paul McBrayer (1928, 29, 30)
Walter McCarty (1994, 95, 96)
Bob McCowan (1969, 72)
Jim McDonald (1960, 61, 62)
James McFarland (1924, 25, 26)
Skip McGaw (1990)
Lawrence McGinnis (1928, 29, 30)
Louis McGinnis (1929, 30, 31)
Dan McHale (Mgr.)
(1998, 99, 2000, 01)
James Mcintosh (1937)
Troy McKinley (1982, 83, 84, 85)
J. McKinney (Mgr.) (1936, 37)
C.F. Meadors (1912)
Jodie Meeks (2007, 08, 09)

181

Ron Mercer (1996, 97)
Hub Metry (Mgr.) (1964, 65)
Brett Miller (Mgr.) (2010, 11)
Darius Miller (2009, 10, 11)
Derrick Miller (1987, 88, 89, 90)
Cameron Mills (1995, 96, 97, 98)
Chris Mills (1989)
Don Mills (1958, 59, 60)
Ray Mills (1955, 56, 57)
Terry Mills (1969, 70, 71)
Stanley Milward (1928, 29, 30)
Will Milward (1924, 25)
Dirk Minniefield (1980, 81, 82, 83)
Terry Mobley (1963, 64, 65)
Nazr Mohammed (1996, 97, 98)
Gayle Mohney (1926)
Bob Moore (Mgr.) (1950, 51, 52)
Caleb Moore (Mgr.) (2000, 01, 02, 03)
Eric Moore (Mgr.) (1989)
Ralph Morgan (1913, 14, 15)
Jonathan Morris (Mgr.) (2005)
Randolph Morris (2005, 06, 07)
Jeff Morrow (Mgr.) (1989, 90, 91, 92)
Tom Moseley (1944)
Ravi Moss (2003, 04, 05, 06)
Kevin Murphy (Mgr.) (1998, 99, 2000)
Zach Murphy (Mgr.) (2005, 06, 07, 08)

N

Cotton Nash (1962, 63, 64)
Alonzo Nelson (1945)
Roger Newman (1961)
C.M. Newton (1951)
Tommy Nichols (1936)
Brad Noe (Mgr.) (2006)
Nertlens Noel (2013)
Paul Noel (1943)
Randy Noll (1970)

O

Lukasz Obrzut (2004,-07)
Dan Omlor (Mgr.) 64)
Bernard Opper 1937, 38, 39)
Daniel Orton (2010)
Hays Owens (1928, 29, 30)

P

Scott Padgett (1995, 97, 98, 99)
Harold Park (Mgr.) (1945)
James Park (1914)
Clyde Parker (1943)
Ed Parker (Mgr.) (1919)
J. Ed Parker (1945, 46, 47)
Jason Parker (2001)
Tom Parker (1970, 71, 72)
Jack Parkinson (1944, 45, 46, 48)
Michael Parks (1990)
Dick Parsons (1959, 60, 61)
Patrick Patterson (2008, 09, 10)
Tom Payne (1971)
Bart Peak (1917)
Leonard Pearson (1950)
John Pelphrey (1989, 90, 91, 92)
Doug Pendygraft (1962)
ES Penick (1943)
Bobby Perry (2004, 05, 06, 07)
Dwight Perry (2007, 08, 09)
Dan Perry (1972)
George Perry (Mgr.) (1954)
Mike Phillips (1975, 76, 77, 78)
Frank Phipps (1927)
Wayne Plummer (1909)
Jarrod Polson (2011 12, 13)
Randy Pool (1968, 69)
Stacey Poole (2011)
Mark Pope (1995, 96)
Michael Porter (2007, 08, 09)
Tommy Porter (1966, 67, 68)
Shelby Post (1908, 09)
Sam Potter (1934)
William Poynz (1921, 23)
Alex Poytress (@013)
Mike Pratt (1968, 69, 70)
R.C. Preston (1911, 12, 13, 14)
Dwight Price (1951)
Jared Prickett (1993, 94, 95, 97)
Tayshaun Prince (1999, 2000, 01, 02)
Linville Puckett (1954)
Larry Pursiful (1960, 61, 62)

R

Frank Ramsey (1951, 52, 54)
Lloyd Ramsey (1941, 42)
Tripp Ramsey (Mgr.) (1976, 77)
Robert Reynolds (1932)
Rodrick Rhodes1993, 94, 95)

A.T. Rice (1923, (24)
Sam Ridgeway (1920, 21)
Andre Riddick (1992, 93, 94, 95)
Carl Riefkin (1923, 24)
Pat Riley (1965, 66, 67)
RN Roark (1904)
Roy Roberts (1962, 63)
Rick Robey (1975, 76, 77, 78)
Al Robinson (1959)
William "Doc" Rodes (1917)
William Rodes (1909, 10)
Andrew Rogers (Mgr) (2010)
Karl Rohs (1925)
Don Rolfes (1963)
Kenneth Rollins (1943, 47, 48)
Rajon Rondo (2005, 06)
Van Buren Ropke (1927)
Gayle Rose (1952, 54, 55)
Harold Ross (1956, 57, 58)
Ben Roth (Mgr) (1915)
Layton Rouse (1938, 39, 40)
Willie Rouse (1954)
Herky Rupp (1961)
Tony Russell (Mgr) (1994, 95, 96, 97)

S

Forest Sale (1931, 32, 33)
Chad Sanders (Mgr)
(2007, 08, 09, 10)
Matt Scherbenske (2008)
Charles Schrader (1914, 17)
Wilber Schu (1944, 45, 46)
Herschel Scott (1913, 14, 15)
Mike Scott (1987, 88, 89)
Jason Seamonds (Mgr) (1998, 99)
Cory Sears (2001, 02)
Jim Server (1915, 16)
Evan Settle (1933, 34)
AP. Shanklin (1918)
Shelby Shanklin (1908)
James Sharpe (1927)
Jeff Sheppard (1994, 95, 96, 98)
Jay Shidler (1977, 78, 79, 80)
Terry Shigg (1987)
Oliver Simmons (1996)
Glenn Sims (Mgr) (1973)
Rekalin Sims (2006)
George Skinner (1933)

Landon Slone (2009)
Bobby Slusher (1959)
Adrian Smith (1957, 58)
Bill Smith (1956, 57, 58)
Doug Smith (Mgr) (2006)
G.J. Smith (1973, 74, 75)

G.K. Smith (1921, 23)
Saul Smith (1998, 99, 00, 01)
Mark Soderberg (1970)
Patrick Sparks (2005, 06)
Carey Spicer (1929, 30, 31)
Bill Spivey (1950, 51)
Vincent Splane (1942)
Carl Staker (1940, 41, 42)
Larry Stamper (1971, 72, 73)
Larry Steele (1969, 70, 71)
Tim Stephens (1977, 78)
Willie Cauley-Stein (2013)
Perry Stevenson (2007, 08, 09, 10)
AJ. Stewart (2008, 09)
Gene Stewart (1967)
Bobby Stilz (1967)
C.P. Sl. John (1904)
Brian Stocker (Mgr) (1994, 95, 96, 97)
Brandon Stockton (2003, 04, 05, 06)
Marvin Stone (2000, 01)
N. Stone (1908)
John Strogh (1945, 48)
Guy Strong (1950)
William Sturgill (1945, 46)
Don Sullivan (Mgr) (1978, 79)
Anthony Summers (Mgr)
(1998, 99, 2000)
Bill Surface (Mgr) (1955)
Sean Sutton (1988, 89)
Todd Svoboda (1993)

T

Todd Tackett (1999, 2000)
Bob Tallent (1966)
Spencer Tatum (Mgr) (1989, 90, 91, 92)
Vincent Tatum (Mgr) (1991, 92)
Bob Taylor (1935)
Alan Theobald (Mgr) (1968)
H.C. Thomas (1918, 19)
Henry Thomas (1991, 92)

185

Irving Thomas (1986, 87)
Roger Thomas (Mgr) (1982, 83)
Sheray Thomas (2004, 05, 06, 07)
Homer Thompson (1937, 38, 39)
Tommy Thompson (Mgr) (1960)
Milton Ticco (1941, 42, 43)
E.J. Tierney (1935)
Clarence Tillman (1979)
Aminu Timberlake (1992, 93)
Jack Tingle (1944, 45, 46, 47)
Carlos Toomer (1991, 92)
Garland Townes (1950)
Bill Trott (1931)
Lou Tsioropoulos (1951, 52, 54)
Jack Tucker (1933, 34, 35)
Wayne Turner (1996, 97, 98, 99)
Melvin Turpin (1981, 82, 83, 84)
Paul Turrell (1935)
William P. Tuttle (1912, 13, 1415)

U

Eiki Umezaki (Mgr) (1989)
Lovell Underwood (1924, 25, 26)

V

Eloy Vargas (2011)
Chuck Verderber (1979, 80, 81, 82)
Frank Vogel (Mgr) (1996)
George Vulich (1944, 45)

W

Antoine Walker (1995, 96)
J. Rice Walker (1936, 37, 38)
Kenny Walker (1983, 84, 85, 86)
John Wall (2010)
Reggie Warford (1976)
LB. Waters (1905)
Robert Watson (1950, 51, 52)
AJ. Weisenberger (1911, 13)
Wylie B. Wendt (1906)
Leo Wenkley (Mgr) (1930)
Clint Wheeler (1971)
Lucian Whitaker (1950, 51, 52)
Waller White (1940, 41, 42)
Don Whitehead (1944)

James Wilhelm (1921)
W.G. Wilkinson (1923)
Adam Williams (2006)
LaVon Williams (77, 78, 79, 80)
Morakinyo Williams (2008)
Maury Wilson (1906, 07, 08)
W.C. Wilson (1913)
Kyle Wiltjer (2013)
Phil Whitt (Trn) (1977)
Sean Woods (1990, 91, 92)
Charles Worthington (1931, 32)
 H.J. Wurtele (1904)

Y

George Yates (1930, 31, 33)
Humzey Yessin (Mgr)
(1946, 47, 48, 49)
RudyYessin (1944)

Z

George Zerfoss (1916, 18)
Karl Zerfoss (1913, 15, 16)
Tom Zerfoss (1914)
Todd Ziegler (1985, 86)

1947-48 Wildcats: Front Row--Coach Adolph Rupp, Johnny Stough, Ralph Beard, Kenny Rollins, Cliff Barker, Dale Barnstable, Assistant Coach Harry Lancaster. Back row—Mgr. Humzey Yessin, Garland Townes, Jim Jordan, Joe Holland, Alex Groza, Wallace Jones, Jim Line, Roger Day, Trainer Bud Berger.

Madison Square Garden, March 23, 1948
Kentucky 58, Baylor, 42

The Bears were determined to slow down the game and play possession ball. They made sure every shot was close and clear; as a result, they took only one chance in the first four minutes of the first half, without making a shot. The Wildcats got off to a 24-7 halftime lead, which Baylor managed to trim to 29-15 at halftime. Baylor later cut the lead to nine points, but the Wildcats went into overdrive and won going away.

Front Row: Coach Adolph Rupp, Jim Line, Cliff Barker, John Stough, Ralph Beard, Joe Hall, Garland Townes, Assistant Coach Harry Lancaster.
Back Row: Dale Barnstable, Walt Hirsch, Wallace Jones, Alex Groza, Bob Henne, Roger Day, Mgr. Humzey Yessin.

Seattle, Wash., March 27, 1949
Kentucky 46, Oklahoma A&M 36

When Alex Groza fouled out with five minutes to play, an overflow crowd of 12,500 at the University of Washington pavilion gave him a standing ovation. The big Wildcat center scored 25 points and controlled the boards. Sports writers unanimously voted him the most valuable player for the second straight Final Four.

Oklahoma A&M utilized its ball-controlled style of play to start with a 5-2 lead. Groza got in gear, scored 15 points and UK led 25-20 at halftime. Although Groza was benched eight minutes with four fouls in the second half, he returned just midway of the period and went out with five fouls five minutes before the gun.

189

Standing: Frank Ramsey, Shelby Linville, Bill Spivey, Roger Layne, Lou Tsioropoulos, Read Morgan. **Seated:** Coach Adolph Rupp, Cliff Hagan, C.M. Newton, Walt Hirsch, Paul Lansaw, Dwight Price, Assistant Coach Harry Lancaster. **Bottom Row:** Lindle Castle, Lucian Whitaker, Bobby Watson, Guy Strong, T. Riddle.

Minneapolis, March 27, 1951
Kentucky 68, Kansas State 58

The Wildcats, cast in the role of underdog for the first time in 10 years trailed Kansas by six points, then lost a two-point lead and went in at the half behind, 29-27.

They Wildcats came out clawing and grabbed a 35-30 lead after two minutes of the second period. When they extended that margin to 54-39 it was all over except the celebrating Spivey led all scorers with 22 points. He also pulled down a game-high 21 rebounds—almost half of UK's total of 45—while Kansas State got just 30.

Front Row: Coach Adolph Rupp, Adrian Smith, John Crigler, Ed Beck, Don Mills, Johnny Cox, Vernon Hatton, Assistant Coach Harry Lancaster.
Second Row: Student Manager Jay Atkerson, Earl Adkins, Billy Smith, Phil Johnson, Bill Cassady, Lincoln Collinsworth and Harold Ross.

Louisville, Ky., March 21, 1958
Kentucky 84, Seattle 72

The Wildcats trailed all the way, once by 11 points, until only six minutes remained in the game. Sophomore Don Mills sank a short hook shot that put UK ahead, 61-60. Johnny Cox immediately followed with a push shot from the circle. Adrian

Smith added a free throw to make it 64-60. Vernon made a free throw but missed the second try; however, grabbed the rebound and fired in a field goal, which gave UK the lead, 67-60 with 3:14 left.

Seattle made one last threat with 3:14 left when it came within 68-65, but Cox hit two free throws to put the game out of Seattle's reach. Seattle's great Elgin Baylor got into early foul trouble, but he finished with 25 points. Hatton led all scorers with 30. Cox scored 24 while Crigler had 12.

Front Row: Coach Joe Hall, Jay Shidler, Dwane Casey, Kyle Macy, Jack Givens, Tim Stephens, Chris Gettelfinger, Truman Claytor, Assistant Coach Dick Parsons.
Second Row: Assistant Trainer Walt McCombs, Manager Don Sullivan, LaVon Williams, Scott Courts, Mike Phillips, Rick Robey, Chuck Aleksinas, Fred Cowan, James Lee, Assistant Coach Leonard Hamilton, Assistant Coach Joe Dean Jr.

St. Louis, March 26, 1978

Kentucky 94, Duke 88

Led by Jack Givens, who scored 41 points, third highest in NCAA Finals history, the big, experienced Wildcats defeated Duke's youthful Blue Devils, 94-88, before a steamy crowd of 18,721 in the Checkerdome. Givens scored 16 of UK's 18 points in the final sixth minutes of the first half, giving UK a 45-38 lead at the break.

Kentucky extended the lead to 66-50, but Duke refused to fold. In the closing seconds, when Hall pulled his veterans from the game, Duke got the deficit down to 92-88. Duke called a time-out with 10 seconds left, but by then Kentucky's regulars were back in the game. The game ended with James Lee taking a pass in the forecourt, eluding Duke's Bob Bender and ending the game with a tremendous dunk.

Front Row: Assistant Coach Delray Brooks, Head Coach Rick Pitino, Allen Edwards, Derek Anderson, Jeff Sheppard, Tony Delk, Anthony Epps, Cameron Mills, Wayne Turner, Associate Coach Jim O'Brien, Assistant Coach Winston Bennett.
Back Row: Equipment Manager Bill Keightley, Administrative Assistant George Barber, Jason Lathrem, Oliver Simmons, Nazr Mohammed, Mark Pope, Walter McCarty, Antoine Walker, Jared Prickett, Ron Mercer, Trainer Eddie Jamiel, Assistant Strength Coach Layne Kaufman, Strength Coach Shaun Brown.

East Rutherford, N. J., April 1, 1996
Kentucky 76, Syracuse 67

After a close opening 10 minutes, the Cats took control when Ron Mercer hit a three-pointer to break a 28-28 tie. Two treys by Tony Delk, one by Mercer and a pair of free throws by Antoine Walker gave UK a 42-33 lead at halftime. Midway through the second half, a lay-up by Mercer started a run of 11 unanswered points that increase the UK lead to 59-46.

The Orangemen eventually pulled within two points (64-62) with 4:46 remaining. A tip-in by Walter McCarty and a trey by Anderson put the Wildcats ahead by seven (69-62). The outscored Syracuse by 7-5 in the last minutes and gave UK its sixth NCAA championship, something that had denied them for 18 years

Front Row: (L-R) Assistant Coach Mike Sutton, Head Coach Orlando "Tubby" Smith, Saul Smith, Cameron Mills, Jeff Sheppard, Wayne Turner, Steve Masiello, Assistant Coach George Felton, Assistant Coach Shawn Finney. **Standing:** Special Assistant Leon Smith, Administrative Assistant Simeon Mars, Equipment Manager Bill Keightley, Ryan Hogan, Heshimu Evans, Scott Padgett, Nazr Mohammed, Jamaal Magloire, Michael Bradley, Myron Anthony, Allen Edwards, Trainer Eddie Jamiel, Strength Coach Tom Boyd.

San Antonio, March30, 1998

195

Kentucky 78, Utah 69

Utah not only out-rebounded the Wildcats, 24-6, in the first half, but also led by 10 (41-31) at halftime. No team had ever come from behind by more than eight points to win a championship game. During one 90-second spree, the Utes used superior rebounding and a 10-0 drive to build a 34-23 lead with 6:52 remaining before halftime.

The Cats were trailing by 10 when Heshimu Evans scored eight quick points. Cameron Mills hit a trey to pull them even at 58-58 at the 7:48 mark. Jeff Sheppard stole the ball and his dunk gave UK a two-point lead, but Utah scored an unanswered six points and regained the lead at 64-60. Mills hit a trey and Sheppard sank a short jumper to give UK the lead for good. The tiring Utes made only one bucket in the final six minutes, missing 11 consecutive shots in one stretch.

Scott Padgett led four Wildcats in double figures with 17 points. Sheppard, named the most outstanding player, had 16, while Anderson and Walker scored 11 each.

Front Row: Kenny Payne, Orlando Antigua, Brian Long, Sam Malone, Doron Lamb, Marquis Teague, Ryan Harrow, Jarrod Polson, John Calipari, John Robic
Second Row: Jon Hood, Michael Kidd-Gilchrist, Terrence Jones, Kyle Wiltjer, Anthony Davis, Eloy Vargas, Darius Miller, Twany Beckham

New Orleans April 2, 2012
Kentucky 67, Kansas 59

The Wildcats defeated in-state rival Louisville, 69-61, to earn a spot in the championship game with Kansas. Doron Lamb led all scorers with 22 points. That included back-to-back 3-pointers that put UK up by 16 with 10 minutes remaining. Marcus Teague added 14 more for UK. The Jayhawks held K's Anthony Davis to six points; however, the big freshman got 16 rebounds, blocked six shots, and got three steals. That earned him most valuable player honors. The win marked Calipari's first and UK's eighth NCAA championship.

Chapter Eleven
Kentucky Hoops Timeline

Feb, 6, 1903
Walter H. Mustaine organizes school's first men's basketball team.

Feb. 18, 1906
UK's first win, over the local YMCA, 11- 10, is sandwiched between losses to Georgetown and Transylvania.

Feb. 18, 1909
Wildcats ensure their first winning season (5-4 record).

Jan. 10, 1910
Athletics Council appoints E. R. Sweetland as athletic director and its first basketball coach.

March 1, 1912
UK 19, Georgetown 18
The victory over Georgetown gives UK a perfect 9-0 record.

Feb. 9, 1918
UK 21, Wesleyan 21
WINCHESTER—Kentucky and Kentucky Wesleyan play to a tie due to a scorer's error.

March 1, 1921
UK 20, Georgia 19
ATLANTA--Designated shooter William King hits a free throw after time expires to give UK the first championship of the first SIAA Tournament. Basil Hayden becomes UK's first All-American in any sport.

Dec. 13, 1924
UK 28, Cincinnati 23

LEXINGTON--Wildcats defeat Cincinnati, in the new 2,800-seat, $100,000 Alumni Gym .Jim McFarland leads all scorers with 10 points.

Dec. 18, 1928
UK 33, Clemson 17
LEXINGTON--The Wildcats defeat Clemson in the first game played under new coach John Mauer, who compiled a 40-14 record during three years at the university.

Dec 21, 1928
UK 43, Miami 42
LEXINGTON--The Wildcats defeat Miami (Ohio in three overtimes.

Jan. 12, 1929
UK 19, Notre Dame 16
SOUTH BEND, Ind.—Kentucky defeats Notre Dame, 19-16, in the first meeting between the two schools. The Irish would win the next seven.

March 21, 1930
The university hires Adolph Rupp, a high school coach in Freeport, Ill., to succeed Johnny Mauer as head basketball and assistant football coach. Freshman basketball player Ellis Johnson is a member of the hiring group.

Dec. 18, 1930
UK 67, Georgetown 19
Kentucky defeats Georgetown, 67-19, for the first of Rupp's 826 wins. Tiger captain Harry Lancaster scores the game's first two points. Ellis Johnson scores the first points for Rupp.

March 3, 1931
UK 27, Maryland 29

ATLANTA--Maryland hits a long shot in the final seconds to defeat UK, in the championship of the Southern Conference Tournament. The Wildcats finish 13-3 in Rupp's first season.

Feb. 28, 1933
UK 46, Mississippi State 27
ATLANTA—Kentucky defeats State, in the championship game of the first tournament held by the newly formed Southeastern Conference. Three Kentuckians—Ellis Johnson, John DeMoisey and Forest Sale are named to the inaugural SEC team.

Feb. 17, 1934
UK 47, Vanderbilt 27
LEXINGTON--The Wildcats establish a national record of 23 consecutive victories.

Feb. 24, 1934
UK 32, Florida 38
ATLANTA—Kentucky takes a 16-0 record into the SEC Tournament, but is upset by Florida, robbing Rupp his first undefeated season.

Jan. 2, 1935
UK 42, Chicago 16
CHICAGO—LeRoy "Big Boy" scores 26 points, to lead UK over the Windy City crew.

Jan. 5, 1935
UK 22, St. John's 23
NEW YORK--In their first trip to Madison Square Garden, the Wildcats lose to St. John's, on a disputed foul call. "We were strangers and they took us in," Rupp said.

Summer, 1935
INDIANAPOLIS, Ind.—Wildcat center LeRoy Edwards, who was named All-America in his sophomore year, called Rupp and

said was married, had a job and would play semi-pro ball and not return to UK.

March 7, 1935
WLAP-Radio airs the first live broadcast of a UK basketball game. The Wilds defeat Xavier, 46-29.

Feb. 26, 1936
KNOXVILLE—After a one-year hiatus, the SEC tournament moved from Atlanta to Knoxville, where the Wildcats defeat Ole Miss, 41-39, but lose to Tennessee, 39-28.

March 1, 1937
UK 39, Tennessee 25
KNOXVILLE--The Wildcats defeat Tennessee, to wins their second SEC Tournament. They place Ralph Carlisle, Warfield Donahue, Walter Hodge and Rice Walker on the all-tournament tea

Dec. 15, 1937
With Rupp bedridden with the flu, Paul McBrayer coaches the Wildcats to a 69-5 win over Berea.

Dec. 29, 1937
UK 40, Pitt 29
NEW ORLEANS—The Wildcats defeat Pittsburgh, in their first Sugar Bowl appearance.

Feb, 14, 1938
UK 35, Marquette 33
LEXINGTON--Joe "Red" Hagan hits a 48-foot shot with 12 seconds left and the Cats defeat Marquette, 35-33, in the first meeting between the two schools. Gov. A. B. "Happy" Chandler drives a nail on the spot in Alumni Gym where the shot was launched.

March 4, 1939
UK 46, Tennessee 38
KNOXVILLE—Bernie Opper leads UK to victory over
Tennessee, in the finals of the SEC Tournament. Opper later won
All-America honors.

March 2, 1940
UK 51, Georgia 43
KNOXVILLE--The Wildcats defeat Georgia for their second
SEC Tournament championship.

Jan. 4, 1941
UK 48, Notre Dame 47
LOUISVILLE—With score apparently tied at 47-47, Kentucky,
and Notre Dame line up to begin the overtime period in the
Armory. However, the official scorer informs the referees that a
scoreboard operator had failed to record a second-half Notre
Dame, and the Irish won 48-47.

March 1, 1941
LOUISVILLE--An Alabama player knocks Lee Huber's last
second shot out of the basket and UK is awarded the goal that
beats the Tide, 39-37. Tennessee beats UK, 36-33, in the
championship game.

Jan. 10, 1942
UK 40, Xavier 39
CINCINNATI--Ermal Allen's two free throws with four seconds
left give UK a 40-39 win over Xavier. "That boy doesn't have
any blood in him," Rupp says. "It's all ice."

Feb. 28, 1942
UK 36, Tennessee 34
LOUISVILLE—Kenny England comes off the bench and scores
13 points and leads UK to a win over Tennessee in the finals of
the SEC Tournament.

March 20, 1942
NEW ORLEANS--The Wildcats win their first NCAA Tournament game, 46-44 over the Illinois "Whiz Kids". They lose to Dartmouth, 47-28, the following night.

Jan. 23, 1943
Kentucky falls behind by 10 points, but Marvin Akers and Melvin Ticco combine for 33 points as Rupp's Wildcats, after seven unsuccessful attempts, defeat Notre Dame, 60-55, in Lexington.

Dec. 40, 1943
NEW YORK—The Wildcat defeat St. John's, 44-38, for their first victory in Madison Square Garden.

March 4, 1944
LOUISVILLE—the Wildcats defeat Tulane, 62-46, for their seventh SEC Tournament title in 11 such events since 1933.

March 22, 1944
NEW YORK—The same St. John's team that Kentucky defeated early in the season defeats the Wildcats, 48-45, in the NIT semi-finals.

Jan. 6, 1945
The Wildcats defeat Arkansas State 75-6. The six points is still a record for fewest points allowed in a single game (since 1938.

March 3, 1945
LOUISVILLE—Kentucky defeats Tennessee, 39-35, for championship of the SEC Tournament.

March 2, 1946

LOUISVILLE—Kentucky defeats LSU, 59-36, for the SEC trophy. The Wildcats win their four games by an average margin of 33.5 points.

Dec. 30, 1946
NEW ORLEANS—Henry Ibo slows down the game and his Oklahoma A&M boys beat the Wildcats, 37-31, in the Sugar Bowl. A&M would win a second straight NCAA title later that season.

March 20, 1946
NEW YORK--Ralph Beard sinks a last-seconds free throw to beat Rhode Island 46-45, in the NIT and give UK its first national championship.

March 1, 1947
LOUISVILLE—Kentucky defeats Tulane, 55-38, to win the SEC Tournament. Five Wildcats, all native Kentuckians—Ralph Beard, Wallace Jones, Joe Holland, Jack Tingle and Kenny Rollins make the all-tournament first team. Groza is a second-team choice.

March 24, 1947
NEW YORK--Watt Misaka (5'8") holds Ralph Beard to two points, his lowest ever, and Utah spoils UK's bid to become back-to-back NIT champions.

Feb. 14, 1948
Ralph Beard hits a 53'9"set shot in a 69-42 win over Tennessee. Team captain Kenny Rollins drives a nail to mark the spot in Alumni Gym.

Jan. 5, 1948
MIAMI, Ohio-Prior to a game with Miami, Adolph Rupp announces a starting lineup of Ralph Beard and Kenny Rollins at guard, Alex Groza at center, and Cliff Barker and Wallace Jones

at forward. That "Fabulous Five" defeats the Redskins, 67-53, that night.

Feb. 14, 1948
Ralph hits a 52 ½-foot shot with one second remaining in the second half of a 69-42 win over Tennessee for the longest field goal in UK history up to that time.

March 20 1948
NEW YORK—In the NCAA semi-finals, Kenny Rollins and Dale Barnstable hold Holy Cross star Bob Cousy to six points and UK defeats the defending national champions, 60-52

March 23, 1948
NEW YORK--UK's "Fabulous Five" defeats Baylor, 58-42, for the school's first NCAA championship.

March 31, 1948
NEW YORK--In what was termed the "Greatest Game of All Time", the Phillips 66ers defeat UK, 43-39, before 18,475 in the Olympic Trials championship game held in MSG.

July 7, 1948
Playing on Stoll Field before the largest crowd (14,000 fans) to see a basketball game in the state of Kentucky, the Wildcats lose an exhibition game to the Phillips Oilers, 50.

Aug. 13, 1948
LONDON--The U. S. Olympic basketball team, featuring UK's "Fabulous Five", defeats France, 64-21, in the championship game. Alex Groza leads all scorers in the tournament.

Feb. 26, 1949
Cliff Barker hits a UK record 63' 7 ½" field goal in 70-37 win over Vanderbilt.'

March 26, 1949
SEATTLE--Ranked No. 1 in AP's first seasonal basketball poll, the Wildcats defeat Oklahoma A&M, 46-36, for their second consecutive NCAA championship.

Dec. 3, 1949
Jim Lines scores 7 points, one shy of the UK record held by Alex Groza, as UK opens the season with a victory 84-61, over Indiana Central.

Jan. 14, 1950
KNOXVILLE--For the first time since 1945, Kentucky loses to an SEC team, falling to Tennessee, 53-66. The Wildcats had won 64 SEC games in a row.

Dec. 1, 1950
Kentucky defeats West Texas State, 73-43, in the first game played in Memorial Coliseum. Eight days later, they dedicate the building with a 70-52 win over Purdue.

Dec. 16, 1950
UK's Bill Spivey outscores Kansas center Clyde Lovellette, 68-39, to win the "Battle of the Giants" in the only game played between Rupp and his old mentor Phog Allen.

Jan. 29, 1951
NEW ORLEANS—Kentucky beats Tulane, 104-68, marking the first time the Wildcats pass the century mark.

March 3, 1951
LOUISVILLE—Vanderbilt defeats the Wildcats, 56-61, ending UK's streak of 26 consecutive wins and seven titles in SEC tournament play.

March 24, 1951

NEW YORK--Shelby Linville scores with 11 seconds remaining to defeat Illinois, 76-74, in MSG and send UK to the Final Four.

March 27, 1951
MINNEAPOLIS--Kentucky defeats Kansas State, 68-58, for a third NCAA title.

Dec. 17, 1951
Cliff and Bobby Watson each score 25 points as the Wildcats defeat St. John's, extending their home winning streak to 100 consecutive games.

Jan. 2, 1952
OWENSBORO, KY.—The Wildcats break their own SEC scoring record with116-58 win over Mississippi. Playing in his hometown, Cliff Hagan makes a school record 16 free throws in a row.

Feb. 11, 1952
NASHVILLE—Cliff Hagan scores 30 points and Frank Ramsey 29 points as the Wildcats defeat Mississippi State, 110-66, to set a Memorial Coliseum scoring record. .

March 1, 1952
NASHVILLE--Cliff Hagan scores 30 points and Frank Ramsey 29 points as the Wildcats defeat Mississippi State, 110-66, in the SEC tournament. . Lou Tsioropoulos scores the winning basket against LSU, 44-43, in the final.

March 22, 1952
RALEGH, N. C.--St. John's beats UK, 57-64 in the NCAA East Regional.

1952-53
SEC & NCAA Suspend UK Season.

Dec. 5, 1953
Cliff Hagan scores a school and SEC record 51 points in a 86-59 victory over Temple as the Wildcats return from a year of suspension. Cawood Ledford broadcasts his first UK game.

Dec. 21-22, 1953
The first University of Kentucky Invitational Tournament (UKIT) features Duke, LaSalle and UCLA. Kentucky defeats Duke, 85-69, and LaSalle, 73-60, in the first University of Kentucky Invitational Tournament. UCLA also participated.

March 9, 1954
NASHVILLE--The Wildcats defeat LSU, 61-56, in a conference playoff game and close the book on its first undefeated season since 1912.

Dec. 22, 1954
Kentucky wins the second annual UKIT, defeating LaSalle, the defending national champion, 63-54.

Jan. 8, 1955
Georgia Tech shocks the Wildcats, 59-58, in Memorial Coliseum, ending UK's national streak of 129 consecutive home victories.

March 5, 1955
Adolph Rupp, in his 25th year as UK coach, is presented a blue and white Cadillac. His Wildcats defeat Tennessee, 104-61, and win the SEC with a 12-2 record.

March 11, 1955
EVANSTON, Ill.,--Marquette defeats UK, 71-79 in the Eastern Regional.

Dec. 10, 1955

Bob Burrow's 34 rebounds ties the school record set by Bill Spivey, but UK loses to Temple, 61-73.

March 17, 1956
IOWA CITY—Host Iowa defeats the Wildcats, 89-77, in the Midwest Regional semi-finals.

Dec. 26, 1956
Kentucky defeats previously undefeated Illinois, 91-57, to win the UKIT.

March 15, 1957
John Brewer hits 8 of 8 free throws down the stretch to preserve UK's win over Pittsburgh, 98-92, in the Mideast Regional at Lexington. Michigan State eliminated UK, 80-68, the following day.

Dec. 7, 1957
Vernon Hatton hits a last-second shot from mid-court to put a game with Temple into the second of three overtimes. He scores UK's last six points as they win, 85-83.

March 21, 1958
LOUISVILLE--Vernon Hatton makes a lay-up with 17 seconds remaining to give the Wildcats a 61-60 win over Temple and a berth in the NCAA championship game.

March 22, 1958
LOUISVILLE--Vernon Hatton's 30 points lead the "Fiddlin' Five" over Seattle, 84-72, in Louisville, as UK claims its fourth NCAA title.

Dec. 15 1958
With Maryland holding a three-point lead with seconds left, UK's Bennie Coffman hits a driving shot and is fouled by

Terrapin center Al Bunge. Coffman makes the free throw and UK goes on to win, 58-56, in overtime.

March 13, 1959
EVANSTON, Ill.—Wildcats blow a 15-point halftime lead and lose to Louisville, 61-76 in the Mideast Regional They finish with a 24-2 record.

Feb. 26, 1960
KNOXVILLE—Wildcat lost at Tennessee, 63-65, taking third place in the conference.

March 9, 1961
KNOXVILLE—After regular SEC champ Mississippi State declines the NCAA Tournament bid, the two teams tied for second-place, Kentucky and Vanderbilt, meet for a playoff. The Wildcats win, 88-67, and subsequently lose to Ohio State, 87-74, in the NCAA Mideast Regional at Louisville.

March 17, 1962
IOWA CITY --For the second straight year Ohio State eliminates UK, 64-74, from the NCAA Tournament.

Dec. 1, 1962
For the first time in 36 years, Kentucky loses its season opener, to Virginia Tech, 77-80 in the Coliseum.

Jan. 7, 1963
NASHVILLE-- Kentucky sets a school record that still stands with 46 throws made on 53 attempts in a 105-82 win over Vanderbilt.

Feb. 2, 1963
Cotton Nash becomes the quickest Wildcat to score 1,000 points as his 14 points in a victory over Florida, 94-71, pushes him past the milestone.

Dec. 31, 1963
NEW ORLEANS--Terry Mobley's shot in the closing seconds of overtime gives UK a win over Duke, 81-79, in the Sugar Bowl championship game.

Jan. 6, 1964
NASHVILLE—John Miller's 25-footer with one second left gives Vanderbilt a victory, 83-85, over UK.

Jan. 18, 1964
Rupp surprises Tennessee with a 1-3-1 zone defense and beats them, 66-57. He described it as a "transitional and shifting man-to-man backed by a hyperbolic paraboloid between the ball and the basket"

Feb. 8, 1964.
Cotton Nash pulls down 30 rebounds in UK's 102-59 rout of Ole Miss. The Wildcats grab 108 rebounds, which still stands as an NCAA single game record.

Feb. 29, 1964
KNOXVILLE—The Wildcats defeat Tennessee, 42-38, for the SEC title.

March 13, 1964
MINNEAPOLIS—An integrated Ohio University team defeats the Cats, 85-69, in the Mideast Regional.

Dec 9, 1964
Louie Dampier scores 37 points in a win, 85-77, over Iowa State. That still stands as a UK record for a guard.

March 1, 1965
Cats defeat Alabama, 76-72, and finish, 15-10, Rupp's worst season up to that time.

March 5, 1966
KNOXVILLE—Undefeated Cats (23-0) lose to Tennessee, 62-69.

March 18, 1966
COLLEGE PARK, Md.—In a match of the two top-ranked teams, No. 1 UK prevails over Duke, 83-79.

March 19, 1966
COLLEGE PARK, Md.--Texas Western upsets "Rupp's Runts", 72-65, in NCAA championship game.

Dec. 22, 1966
Louie Dampier hits all 14 of his free throw attempt to tie UK's record for free throws in a game. Oregon State is the victim, 96-66, in the UKIT first round.

Feb. 18, 1966
STARKVILLE—Kentucky beats Mississippi State, 103-74, and Adolph Rupp passes Western Kentucky's Ed Diddle to become second (with 260 victories) to Phog Allen on the all-time winning list.

Dec. 2, 1967
Mike Casey scores 28 points, most ever by a first-year player, as UK defeats Michigan, 96-79.

Dec. 10, 1967
Bernie Shively, UK's longtime athletic director dies at his home.

Jan. 27, 1968
BATON ROUGE—When UK defeats LSU, 121-95, it is believed that Adolph Rupp became college basketball's all-time winningest coach. Years later, it was discovered that Rupp had

achieved that feat on Feb. 18, 1967, with a103-74 win over Mississippi State.

March 16, 1968
Dave Sorenson hits a medium jump shot and Ohio State defeats UK, 81-82, in the Mideast Regional final at Lexington.

Dec. 14, 1968
PHILADELPHIA--The Wildcats hit their first 11 field goal attempts and first nine free throws, scoring 31 consecutive points in a 102-78 victory over Pennsylvania.

Jan. 13, 1969
UK defeats Georgia, 88-68, and becomes the first team in college basketball to win 1,000 games.

Feb. 22, 1969
Led by Dan Issel's 36 points and nine rebounds, the Wildcats defeat LSU, 103-89. Pete Maravich scores 45 for the Tigers.

March 13, 1969
MADISON, Wis.—Al McGuire's Marquette defeats UK, 74-81 in the Mideast Regional.

April 13, 1969
SPRINGFIELD, Mass.—Adolph is enshrined into the Naismith Memorial Basketball Hall of Fame.

June. 9, 1969
Tom Payne, a 7-foot All-American from Louisville, becomes the first black basketball player to sign with UK.

Feb. 7, 1970
OXFORD, Miss—Dan Issel scores 53 points in a 120-85 victory over Ole Miss to beat Cliff Hagan's record of 51 against Temple

in 1951. Issel also broke Cotton Nash's career scoring record of 1770 points.

Feb. 21, 1970
BATON ROUGE, La.—"Pistol" Pete Maravich scores 64 points, most ever by a UK opponent, but his LSU team loses to UK, 1121-105. LSU never beat UK while Pete was there.

Feb. 28, 1970
Dan Issel becomes UK's first player to score 2,000 career points as UK defeats Vanderbilt, 90-86.

March 18, 1970
Columbus, Ohio--Dan Issel scores his 2,138th point, a UK record, but the Wildcats lose to Jacksonville, 100-106, in Mideast Regional.

Dec. 1, 1970
EVANSTON, Ill.—Tom Payne becomes the first black scholarship player to compete for UK in a varsity basketball game. He scores 14 points while Tom Parker leads UK with 24 in a 115-100 victory over Northwestern.

Dec. 12, 1970
BLOOMINGTON--Tom Parker scores 24 points and UK defeats Indiana, 95-93, in overtime.

Feb. 19-21 1971
A hospitalized Adolph Rupp stays home while his team loses to Florida and defeats Alabama on the road.

March 18, 1971
ATHENS, Ga.--Jim McDaniels scores 35 points and grabs 11 rebounds as Western Kentucky crushes UK, 107-83, in the Mideast Regional.

Jan. 22, 1972
Jim Andrews hits a last-second shot and
Kentucky defeats Tennessee, 72-70, in Lexington. Two months
later, the Wildcats close Rupp's last regular season with a 67-66
win over the Vols in Knoxville.

March 18, 1972
DAYTON--Adolph Rupp coaches his last game at UK, a 54-73
loss to Florida State in the Mideast Regional.

April 1, 1972
Joe B. Hall replaces Adolph Rupp as UK head coach.

Dec. 2, 1972
Coach Hall has a successful debut as his Wildcats defeat
Michigan State, 75-66. UK finishes 22-8 and wins the SEC
championship.

Feb. 19, 1973
ATHENS, Ga.--Kevin Grevey's 40-point game ties him with Bill
Spivey for the most points scored in a game by a UK sophomore.
UK WINS, 90-86.

March 4, 1974
Faced with the prospect of their first losing season since 1927,
the 12-13 Wildcats defeat Mississippi State, 108-69.

Dec. 7, 1974
BLOOMINGTON, Ind.—The Hoosiers add insult to injury when
Bobby Knight cuffs Joe B. Hall during IU's 98-74 rout of the
Wildcats.

March 22, 1975
DAYTON--The Cats upset No. 1 Indiana, 92-90, in the Mideast
Regional final. Nine days later, they lose to UCLA, 92-85, in the
NCAA championship game at San Diego.

March 31, 1975
San Diego—John Wooden closes out a Hall of Fame career by leading UCLA to a85- 92 win over the Wildcats in the NCAA championship game.

March 8, 1976
The Wildcats come from behind to defeat Mississippi State, 94-93, in overtime in their last game in Memorial Coliseum.

March 13, 1976
NEW YORK—For the first time in 26 years, UK plays in the NIT. James Lee's team-high 20 points lead the Wildcats to a 67-61 win over Niagara.

March 21, 1976
NEW YORK--Kentucky wins its second NIT championship by defeating North Carolina-Charlotte, 71-67, in MSG.

Nov. 27, 1976
Rick Robey scores the first goal in the new Rupp Arena and the Wildcats defeat Wisconsin, 72-64.

Jan. 3, 1977
Kentucky defeats Georgia, 64-59, in the first overtime game played in Rupp Arena.

March 5, 1977
KNOXVILLE—Tennessee beats UK, 79-81, ties the Cats for SEC crown and represents the conference in NCAA play. Kentucky receives at-large bid.

March 17, 1977
COLLEGE PARK--Truman Claytor makes 13 of 15 shots and finishes with 29 points as Kentucky beats VMI, 93-78, in the

second round of the NCAA Tournament. Two nights later, North Carolina defeats UK, 79-72, in the East Regional finals.

Dec. 10, 1977
Adolph Rupp dies of cancer in Lexington as UK's top-ranked Cats defeat Kansas, 73-68, on "Adolph Rupp Night" in Allen Field House on Naismith Drive in Lawrence, Kansas

Jan. 29, 1977
TUSCALOOSA--Rick Robey's two free throws give UK the lead for good in a tightly fought 87-85 victory over the Tide.

March 27, 1978
ST. LOUIS-Jack Givens scores 41 points and UK defeats Duke, 94-88, for the school's fifth NCAA title.

May 1, 1978
SPRINGFIELD, Mass.—Former Wildcat Cliff Hagan becomes UK's second inductee into the Naismith Basketball Hall of Fame.

Dec. 9, 1978
The Wildcats trail Kansas by six points with 31 seconds to play. Dwight Anderson scores back to-back baskets. Then he steals the ball and feeds it to Kyle Macy for a tying jump shot. Macy hits a technical .when a Jayhawk calls an illegal time out.

Jan. 18, 1978
STARKVILLE—Freshman Dwight Anderson makes a UK-record 18 free throws, but Mississippi State defeats the Cats, 63-61.

Feb. 28-March 3
BIRMINGHAM, Ala.—After a 27-year hiatus, the SEC holds a postseason tournament. Tennessee defeats UK, 69-75, in overtime for the championship.

217

Dec. 12, 1979
LAWRENCE, Kan.--Kyle Macy scores three points in the final four seconds of overtime to give UK a 57-56 win over Kansas.

Dec. 15, 1979
The Wildcats hold Indiana to just 19 second-half points and defeat the top-ranked Hoosiers, 69-58.

Feb. 24, 1980
BATON ROUGE--Kyle Macy's jumper give UK a 76-74 win over LSU in SEC title game.

March 13, 1980
Duke defeats UK, 55-54, in the Mideast Regional in Rupp Arena. Kyle Macy bows out with 1,411 points and 470 assists at UK.

Dec. 6 & 13, 1980
Kentucky defeats Ohio State, Indiana and Kansas, back-to-back.

March 15, 1981
TUSCALOOSA—UAB upsets UK, 62-69 in NCAA second round.

Fall, 1981
A stress fracture will keep Sam Bowie out of action for two seasons.

March 11, 1982
NASHVILLE—Middle Tennessee State shocks the Wildcats, 50-44, in the NCAA first round.

May 3, 1982
SPRINGFIELD, Mass.—Frank Ramsey is enshrined in the Basketball Hall of Fame.

March 26, 1983
KNOXVILLE--Louisville defeats UK, 80-68, in overtime to earn a trip to the Final Four. It is the first meeting between the schools in 24 years.

March 10, 1984
NASHVILLE--Kenny Walker hits a shot at the buzzer that gives UK a 51-49 win over Auburn. It is UK's SEC first tournament championship since the event was renewed in 1979. When Charles Barkley was asked later if he cried after Walker's basket, the Auburn star said, "Like a baby".

Jan. 22, 1984
UK's "Twin Towers—Sam Bowie and Melvin Turpin—control the boards (52-45) and hold Houston's Akeem Alajuwon to 14 points as UK wins, 74-67, at home.

March 22, 1984
Winston Bennett's three-point play with 13 seconds remaining propels UK past Louisville, 72-67, and into the region final.

March 31, 1984
SEATTLE--Georgetown outscores Kentucky, 23-2, at the start of the second half and defeats the Wildcats, 53-40, in a Final Four semi-final.

March 22, 1985
DENVER--Joe B. Hall announces his retirement after UK loses to St. John's, 70-86, in the NCAA West Regional.

Nov. 22, 1985
Eddie Sutton coaches his first game at Kentucky, a 77-58 win over Northwestern (La.) State.

March 16, 1986

CHARLOTTE, N. C.—Kenny Walker hits all 11 shots he attempts in a 71-64 win over Western Kentucky in the NCAA second round.

March 22, 1986
ATLANTA—Kentucky defeated LSU three times during the season, but fall to the Tigers, 57-59, in the regional finals.

Dec. 27, 1986
LOUISVILLE--The Wildcats shoot 54.2 percent from the field (32 of 59), hit 11 of 17 three-pointers, and out-rebound the Cards, 41-33, in Freedom Hall. Freshman Rex Chapman scores 26 points and the Cats roll, 85-51.

Feb. 29, 1987
Richard Madison's basket with eight seconds remaining seals UK's 76-75 upset of No. 12 Oklahoma.

Dec. 12, 1987
Cedric Jenkins tips in a missed shot to give UK a 76-75 win over Louisville.

March 13, 1988
BATON ROUGE—Rex Chapman scores 23 points and earns MVP honors as UK defeats Georgia, 62-57, for the SEC Tournament title.

March 24, 1988
BIRMINGHAM—Villanova defeats UK, 80-74, in the South regional semi-finals.

April, 1988
Emery Air Freight envelope intended for father of UK player Chris Mills "pops open," revealing $1,000 in 50-dollar bills; the resulting scandal will scatter coaches and players to the wind and

bring down athletic director Cliff Hagan, a UK icon.

Dec. 27, 1988
Mills records UK's first -- and only triple-double -- 19 points, 10 rebounds, and 10 assists -- in an 85-77 victory over Austin Peay.

March 5, 1989
Richie Farmer scored a trey at the buzzer and the Wildcats defeat Ole Miss, 70-69.

March 10, 1989
KNOXV ILLE--Kentucky closes the season with a 63-77 loss to Vanderbilt in an opening round of the SEC Tournament. The 13-19 record is UK's first losing mark in 61 seasons.

March 19, 1989
The university accepts the resignation of Eddie Sutton as basketball coach.

May 19, 1989
The NCAA places Kentucky's basketball program on probation.

June 2, 1989
Rick Pitino accepts the challenge of rebuilding the shattered UK basketball program.

Nov. 28, 1989
Reggie Hanson scores 24 points and the Wildcats defeat Ohio, 76-73, in Rick Pitino's debut as head coach.

Dec. 9, 1989
LAWRENCE, Kan.—Kansas defeats Kentucky, 95-150. The 245 points are the most ever scored in a UK game and the 150 points is the most ever allowed by a UK team.

Feb. 15, 1990
Kentucky upsets an LSU team, 100-95, that features Shaquille O'Neal and Chris Jackson.

June, 1990
Rick Pitino hires Bernadette Locke, a former assistant for the Georgia Lady Bulldogs basketball team, to his coaching staff at UK. However, she was not, as claimed, the first woman to hold such a post on a men's team.

Feb. 15, 1991
Kentucky built a 23-point lead in the first half over LSU's ninth-ranked team and held on for dear life as Chris Jackson shot the visitors within two points of the Cats when time ran out.

March 2, 1991
Kentucky ends its probation by defeating Auburn, 114-93, before 24,310 at Rupp Arena.

March 15, 1992
Eligible for post-season play for the first time in three years, UK dominates Alabama, 80-54, to win its 16th SEC Championship.

March 28, 1992
PHILADELPHIA—In the East Regional final, Duke defeats the Wildcats, 104-103, in overtime on Christian Laettner's last-second shot. UK's legendary Cawood "Voice of the Wildcats" Ledford retires after that game.

April 3, 1993
NEW ORLEANS--Michigan defeats Kentucky, 81-78, in overtime in the NCAA semi-finals, ending UK's season 30-4. Wildcat star Jamal Mashburn turns pro after that season.

May 10, 1993

SPRINGFIELD—Dan Issel is inducted into the Basketball Hall of Fame.

Dec. 8, 1993
Travis Ford establishes a UK record with 15 assists in a 107-78 win over Eastern Kentucky.

Dec. 17, 1993
Rodney Dent ties a school record when he hits all 12 of his field goal attempts in a 97-61 win over Morehead State.

Dec. 23, 1993
Jeff Brassow's put-back gives UK a last-second win in the Maui Invitational championship game.

Feb. 15, 1994
BATON ROUGE--The Cats trail by 31 points at 15:34, but they connect on 11 three-pointers and defeat LSU, 99-95, for their biggest comeback win ever.

March, 1994
Travis Ford equals Kyle Macy's UK and SEC single-season mark for free-throw shooting accuracy with a 91.2 percent success rate (103-113)

March 12, 1995
ATLANTA--The Cats rally from 19 points back to edge defending champion Arkansas, 95-93, in overtime for the SEC Tournament championship.

March 2, 1996
A 101-63 win over Vanderbilt gives the Cats a 16-0 sweep of the SEC. UK becomes the first team in 40 years to finish with a perfect record in the SEC.

April 1, 1996

EAST RUTHERFORD--The Wildcats squash a late Syracuse rally and win (76-67) their sixth NCAA title. Tony Delk's seven treys ties an NCAA Finals record. The Cats finish, 34-2.

March 31, 1997
INDIANAPOLIS--Without the services of Derek Anderson, the Wildcats advance all the way to the NCAA championship, where they lose to Arizona, 84-79, in overtime. It was Rick Pitino's final game as UK coach.

May 12, 1997
The university hires Orlando "Tubby" Smith as its new basketball coach.

Nov. 20, 1997
The Wildcats defeat Kyle Macy's Morehead Eagles, 88-49, to inaugurate the Tubby Smith era at Kentucky.

Jan. 27, 1998
NASHVILLE--With time running out and UK in a 61-61 deadlock at Vanderbilt, Nazr Mohammad hits a running one-hand shot from 10 feet away to give the Wildcats their ninth straight win.

March 28, 1998
SAN ANTONIO--The Wildcats rally from a 10-point second-half deficit behind the clutch shooting of Jeff Sheppard, Cameron Mills, and Scott Padgett to beat Stanford, 86-85, in a Final Four semi-final.

March 30, 1998
SAN ANTONIO--The "Comeback Cats" rally from a 10-point halftime deficit to defeat Utah, 78-69, winning UK's second national title in two years, its seventh overall.

Dec. 8, 1999

LOUISVILLE--Scott Padgett scores eight of his 17 points in overtime and the Cats defeat Indiana, 70-61, in Freedom Hall.

Jan. 12, 1999
A three-pointer by Brandon Wharton with 1:09 left gives Tennessee a 47-46 win, their first in Lexington since 1979.

March 14, 1999
Behind Scott Padgett's 29-point, 10-rebound performance, the Wildcats overcome a five-point deficit with 1:29 left to beat Kansas, 92-88, in overtime and advance in the regional.

March, 1999
ST. LOUIS--SEC Tournament champion UK wins three games in the NCAA Tournament before losing to Michigan State, 66-73, in St. Louis. Wayne Turner scores five points and eight assists against Michigan State in his record 151st game as a Wildcat.

March 16, 2000
CLEVELAND, Ohio—Tayshaun Prince hits a three-pointer with: 07 left in regulation and the Cats beat St. Bonaventure, 85-80, in a first round NCAA game.

March 18, 2000
CLEVELAND—Syracuse eliminates the Cats, 50-52 in the second round of NCAA play. Jamaal Magloire completes his UK career with a school-record 268 blocked shots, eclipsing Melvin Turpin by 42 rejections.

Sept. 5, 2001
Cawood Ledford dies at his home in Harlan.

Oct. 13, 2000
SPRINGFIELD—The Basketball Hall of Fame enshrines C. M. Newton.

Nov. 9, 2001
NEW YORK--St. John's defeats UK, 62-61, on official's (later admitted) error in Coaches vs. Cancer Classic in MSG. UCLA defeats the Cats, 97-92 in overtime the following night.

March 22, 2001
Philadelphia--Co-SEC champ UK loses to USC, 76-80, in East Regional.

Dec. 8, 2001
Tayshaun Prince hits five straight three's and UK defeats North Carolina, 79-59, in Rupp.

Dec. 18, 2001
MEADOWLANDS--Kentucky leads No. 1 Duke, 78-77, with 17.6 seconds to play, but Devils escape with a thrilling 95-92 overtime victory.

Dec. 29, 2001
Tayshaun Prince scores 18 points as Kentucky defeats Louisville, 82-62, spoiling Rick Pitino's return to Rupp Arena.

Jan. 5, 2002
STARKVILLE--The Cats lead Mississippi State by 20 in the first half at Starkville, but the Bulldogs win, 74-69, in overtime.

Jan. 12, 2002
COLUMBIA, S.C.--Cliff Hawkins' runner with 3.4 seconds remaining beats South Carolina, 51-50.

March 16, 2002
ST. LOUIS—Tayshaun Prince scores 41 points against Tulsa in UK'S 87-82 win in an NCAA second round game.

March 22, 2002

SYRACUSE--Wildcats cut top-ranked Maryland's lead to 66-63 in NCAA Regional, but lose, 68-78, to the eventual national champions.

Keith Bogans is SEC Player of the Year in 2003.

March 16, 2003
NEW ORLEANS—Cats defeat Mississippi State, 64-57, to sweep both the SEC regular season and conference tournament. It marks the first time the feat has been accomplished in 51 seasons.

Dec. 6, 2003
ANAHEIM--Eric Daniels scores 14 points and UK defeats UCLA, 52-50, in the John Wooden Classic.

Dec. 13, 2003
DETROIT--Kentucky defeats Michigan State, 79-74, before a world record basketball crowd of 78,129 at Ford Field, home of the Lions.

March 29, 2003
COLUMBUS, Ohio--Cats lose to Marquette, 69-83, in Mideast
Regional.

Jan. 13, 2004
STARKVILLE--Eric Daniels grabs a tipped desperation pass out
of the air and lays it in as time expires and UK beats Mississippi
State, 67-66.

Jan. 20, 2004
KNOXVILLE--Chuck Hayes scores off his own miss with 3:49
left and UK defeats Tennessee, 69-68, in overtime to UK keep
alive UK's streak of 10 consecutive conference wins on the road.

March 14, 2004
LEXINGTON--East champs Cats defeat Florida, 89-73, for SEC
Tournament title.

March 21, 2004
COLUMBUS, Ohio--No. 1 seeded Wildcats lose to UAB, 75-76,
in NCAA second round.

April 6, 2007'
UK names Billy Clyde Gillispie as head basketball coach before
more than 4,000 at a pep rally.

Nov. 6, 2007
Kentucky defeats Central Arkansas, 67-40 as Billie Gillispie
makes his debut as UK coach

March 31, 2008
Longtime UK basketball equipment manager Bill Keightly,
affectionately known as "Mr. Wildcat", dies in Cincinnati. He
was 81.

Jan. 13, 2009

Knoxville--Jodie Meeks scores 54 points in a 90-72 win over Tennessee. That broke Dan Issel's record of 53 vs. Ole Miss in 1970.

April 1, 2009
UK hires John Calipari as the 22nd coach of the Basketball Wildcats.

Dec. 21. 2009
Kentucky defeats Drexel 88-44 to become the first program in college basketball to reach the 2,000th victory mark.

John Wall was SEC Player of The Year in 2010

June 24, 2010
UK makes history again by placing five players in the first round of the NBA draft. John Wall became the first Wildcat ever named the No. 1 pick when selected by the Washington Wizards. Other Wildcats selected were DeMarcus Cousins, fifth by

Sacramento; Patrick Patterson, 14th by Houston; Eric Bledsoe, 18th by Oklahoma City, and Daniel Orton by Orlando.

April 2, 2011
Kentucky makes its 14th Final Four appearance, losing to eventual champion Connecticut, 55-56,

2010-2011 Recruiting Class
For the second straight season, UK lands the nation' top recruiting class. The signees were guards Stacey Poole, Doron Lamb, Brandon Knight, and forwards Enes Kanter, Terence Jones, and Elos Vargas.

November 11, 2011
Kentucky defeats Marist, 108-58, in the season opener to secure the 34th consecutive win under Coach Calipari and set a new scoring record in the arena.

March 4, 2012
Kentucky closes the 2011-2012 season with a 74-59 win over Florida capping a perfect 16-0 run through the SEC. for the third time.

April 2, 2012
Kentucky defeats Kansas, 67-59, for the school's eighth NCAA championship.

2012-2013 Recruiting Class
Nerlens Noel, Willie Cauley-Stein, Archie Goodman, Alex Poyntress, Kyle Wiltjer

March 15, 2013

Nerlens Noel, a freshman who suffered a knee injury in February, has declared for the NBA draft. Archie Goodwin, a freshman team mate, declared a few days earlier.

Nerlens Noel

Archie Goodwin

2013-2014 Recruiting Class
Julius Randle, PF, 6-9, 250, Plano, (TX)
Aaron Hamilton, SG, 6-4, 200, Travis Richmond (TX)
Andrew Hamilton, PG 6-4, 200, Travis Richmond (TX)
Marcus Lee, PF, 6-9, 215, Antioch, (CA)
James Young, SG, 6-6, 200, Troy, (MI)
Dakari Johnson, C, 6-10, 250, Montverde, (FL)
Derek Willis, SG, 6-9, 200, Mount Washington, (KY)
Dominique Hawkins, Richmond (Madison Central)

2012 NBA Draft

Round 1	Pick 1	Anthony Davis	New Orleans Hornets
Round 1	Pick 2	Michael Kidd-Gilchrist	Charlotte Bobcats
Round 1	Pick 18	Terrence Jones	Houston Rockets
Round 1	Pick 29	Marquis Teague	Chicago Bulls
Round 2	Pick 12	Doron Lamb	Milwaukee Bucks
Round 2	Pick 16	Darius Miller	New Orleans Hornets

2011 NBA Draft

Round 1	Pick 3	Enes Kanter	Utah Jazz
Round 1	Pick 8	Brandon Knight	Detroit Pistons
Round 2	Pick 15	Josh Harrellson	New Orleans Hornets
Round 2	Pick 23	DeAndre Liggins	Orlando Magic

2010 NBA Draft

Round 1	Pick 1	John Wall	Washington Wizards
Round 1	Pick 5	DeMarcus Cousins	Sacramento Kings

Round 1	Pick 14	Patrick Patterson	Houston Rockets
Round 1	Pick 18	Eric Bledsoe	Oklahoma City Thunder
Round 1	Pick 29	Daniel Orton	Orlando Magic

2009 NBA Draft

Round 2	Pick 11	Jodie Meeks	Milwaukee Bucks

2008 NBA Draft

Round 2	Pick 28	Joe Crawford	Los Angeles Lakers

2006 NBA Draft

Round 1	Pick 21	Rajon Rondo	Phoenix Suns

2003 NBA Draft

Round 2	Pick 14	Keith Bogans	Milwaukee Bucks

2002 NBA Draft

Round 1	Pick 23	Tayshaun Prince	Detroit Pistons

2000 NBA Draft

Round 1	Pick 19	Jamaal Magloire	Charlotte Hornets

1999 NBA Draft

| Round 1 | Pick 28 | Scott Padgett | Utah Jazz |

1998 NBA Draft

| Round 1 | Pick 29 | Nazr Mohammed | Utah Jazz |

1997 NBA Draft

| Round 1 | Pick 6 | Ron Mercer | Boston Celtics |
| Round 1 | Pick 13 | Derek Anderson | Cleveland Cavaliers |

1996 NBA Draft

Round 1	Pick 6	Antoine Walker	Boston Celtics
Round 1	Pick 16	Tony Delk	Charlotte Hornets
Round 1	Pick 19	Walter McCarty	New York Knicks
Round 2	Pick 23	Mark Pope	Indiana Pacers

1994 NBA Draft

| Round 2 | Pick 4 | Rodney Dent | Orlando Magic |

1993 NBA Draft

| Round 1 | Pick 4 | Jamal Mashburn | Dallas Mavericks |

1988 NBA Draft

| Round 1 | Pick 8 | Rex Chapman | Charlotte Hornets |

Round 3	Pick 1	Robert Lock	Los Angeles Clippers
Round 3	Pick 10	Ed Davender	Washington Bullets
Round 3	Pick 14	Winston Bennett	Cleveland Cavaliers

1987 NBA Draft

Round 5	Pick 2	James Blackmon	New Jersey Nets

1986 NBA Draft

Round 1	Pick 5	Kenny Walker	New York Knickerbockers
Round 5	Pick 22	Roger Harden	Los Angeles Lakers

1984 NBA Draft

Round 1	Pick 2	Sam Bowie	Portland Trail Blazers
Round 1	Pick 6	Mel Turpin	Washington Bullets
Round 4	Pick 11	Dickie Beal	Atlanta Hawks
Round 6	Pick 11	Jim Master	Atlanta Hawks
Round 8	Pick 1	Tom Heitz	Indiana

Pacers

1983 NBA Draft

Round 2	Pick 9	Dirk Minniefield	Dallas Mavericks
Round 3	Pick 20	Derrick Hord	Cleveland Cavaliers
Round 6	Pick 18	Charles Hurt	Milwaukee Bucks

1982 NBA Draft

| Round 7 | Pick 7 | Chuck Verderber | Chicago Bulls |

1981 NBA Draft

| Round 6 | Pick 12 | Fred Cowan | Houston Rockets |

1980 NBA Draft

| Round 5 | Pick 9 | LaVon Williams | Cleveland Cavaliers |
| Round 9 | Pick 4 | Jay Shidler | Chicago Bulls |

1979 NBA Draft

| Round 1 | Pick 22 | Kyle Macy | Phoenix Suns |
| Round 6 | Pick 3 | Truman Clayton | Detroit Pistons |

1978 NBA Draft

| Round 1 | Pick 3 | Rick Robey | Indiana Pacers |

Round 1	Pick 16	Jack Givens	Atlanta Hawks
Round 2	Pick 17	James Lee	Seattle Super Sonics
Round 3	Pick 1	Mike Phillips	New Jersey Nets

1977 NBA Draft

| Round 2 | Pick 2 | Larry Johnson | Buffalo Braves |

1975 NBA Draft

Round 1	Pick 18	Kevin Grevey	Washington Bullets
Round 2	Pick 18	Jimmy Dan Conner	Phoenix Suns
Round 3	Pick 13	Bob Guyette	KC-Omaha Kings
Round 7	Pick 5	Mike Flynn	Philadelphia 76ers

1973 NBA Draft

| Round 7 | Pick 4 | Jim Andrews | Seattle Supersonics |

1972 NBA Draft

| Round 6 | Pick 3 | Tom Parker | Cleveland Cavaliers |
| Round 10 | Pick 3 | Kent Hollenbeck | Detroit |

Pistons

1971 NBA Draft

Round 3	Pick 2	Larry Steele	Portland Trail Blazers
Round 10	Pick 11	Jim Dinwiddie	Philadelphia 76ers
Round 11	Pick 1	Mike Casey	Cleveland Cavaliers

1970 NBA Draft

Round 8	Pick 3	Dan Issel	Detroit Pistons
Round 8	Pick 11	Mike Casey	Chicago Bulls

1969 NBA Draft

Round 10	Pick 12	Phil Argento	Los Angeles Lakers

1968 NBA Draft

Round 5	Pick 10	Thad Jaracz	Boston Celtics
Round 9	Pick 13	Cliff Berger	Milwaukee Bucks

1967 NBA Draft

Round 1	Pick 7	Pat Riley	San Diego Rockets
Round 4	Pick 7	Lou Dampier	Cincinnati

Royals

1966 NBA Draft

Round 3	Pick 4	Tommy Kron	St. Louis Hawks

1964 NBA Draft

Round 2	Pick 5	Cotton Nash	Los Angeles Lakers

1962 NBA Draft

Round 8	Pick 1	Larry Pursiful	Chicago Zephyrs

1961 NBA Draft

Round 5	Pick 4	Bill Lickert	Los Angeles Lakers
Round 7	Pick 5	Roger Newman	Syracuse Nationals
Round 13	Pick 1	Ned Jennings	New York Knicks

1960 NBA Draft

Round 4	Pick 8	Sid Cohen	Boston Celtics
Round 6	Pick 8	George Newman	Boston Celtics
Round 7	Pick 5	Bernie Kauffman	Syracuse Nationals
Round 18	Pick 1	Don Mills	Cincinnati

Royals

1959 NBA Draft

Round 4	Pick 6	John Cox	New York Knicks

1958 NBA Draft

Round 2	Pick 2	Vern Hatton	Cincinnati Royals
Round 4	Pick 4	John Cox	New York Knicks
Round 15	Pick 1	Bill Smith	Cincinnati Royals

1957 NBA Draft

Round 10	Pick 4	Jerry Calvert	Philadelphia Warriors

1956 NBA Draft

	Jerry Bird	Minneapolis Lakers
	Bob Burrow	Rochester Royals
	Phil Grawemeyer	Minneapolis Lakers

1955 NBA Draft

Round 5	Bill Evans	Rochester Royals

1953 NBA Draft

	Cliff Hagan	Boston Celtics

	Frank Ramsey	Boston Celtics
	Lou Tsioropoulos	Boston Celtics

1952 NBA Draft

	Bobby Watson	Milwaukee Hawks
	Lucian Whitaker	Indianapolis Olympians

1950 NBA Draft

	Dale Barnstable	Boston Celtics
	Jim Line	Indianapolis Olympians

1949 NBA Draft

	Cliff Barker	Indianapolis Olympians
	Ralph Beard	Chicago Stags
	Alex Groza	Indianapolis Olympians

1948 NBA Draft

	Wallace Jones	Washington Capitols

Joe Holland	<u>Baltimore Bullets</u>
Jack Parkinson	<u>Washington Capitols</u>
Kenny Rollin	<u>Fort Wayne Pistons</u>

1947 NBA Draft

Jack Tingle	<u>Washington Capitols</u>

Wm. Russell Rice Biography

Born, Paintsville, Ky., 11/07/24, son of Russell Ganes and Alpha Bowe Rice, both of Johnson County, Ky. Moved to Van Lear at an early age.

Played three sports at Van Lear High School. Attended Army Signal Corps School March 1942 until October, 1942. Served in U.S. Marine Corps 1943-45. (two years in South Pacific). Started as radar specialist with 4th AAA Bn. on Guadalcanal; ended in H&S Co., 28th "Flag-Raising" Regiment, 5th. Mar. Div. in Hilo, Hawaii; wrote letters to families of regimental Marines killed on Iwo Jima. With first troops ashore at Sasebo, Kyushu, Japan.

Attended Kentucky Wesleyan College 1947; University of Kentucky `1948-51. B.A. in Journalism. Played baseball (catcher) as freshman at Wesleyan. Sports Editor Seminar at Columbia University 1967.

Worked truck mines in the Garrett-Lackey-Wayland area during summer vacations and holidays in late '40s to supplement attending college on the GI Bill—Shot, loaded, laid track, timbered, pulled pillars; "Load Sixteen tons and what do you get?"

m. Doris Marie Thacker, of Lackey, Ky., in Lexington Jan. 5, 1951; lost her to Alzheimer's in August 2005. Four children, six granddaughters, four great grandchildren.

1951-52—City Editor, Whitesburg (KY), "Mountain Eagle"
1952-53—City Editor, "Hazard (Ky.), Herald".
1953-62—The 'Lexington Leader: 'Police reporter, court reporter, investigative reporter;

(Traveling companion of John Robsion, Republican candidate for governor of Kentucky during his campaign vs. Bert Combs). Also served as Business Page Editor, Farm Page Editor, Church Page Editor, Kentucky correspondent for Religious News Service; Tobacco Magazine; and Time/Life/Fortune magazines. Wrote column, "Sporting Trails" for the Leader.

On special assignment to congressional tobacco hearings in Washington, school bus wreck near Prestonsburg, and mine strikes in east Kentucky.

Wrote series of stories on need for doctors in east Kentucky that appeared in The Leader, which bound them in booklet form and presented same to the Kentucky General Assembly in support of the proposed Chandler Medical Center. Nominated for Pulitzer Prize.

1962-67—Sports Editor, The Lexington Leader.
1967-68—Assistant sports information director, U of Ky.
1968-1987—UK Sports Information Director
1989—Retired as Assistant Athletic Director.
1990—Chief writer and production manager, Collegiate Collection. (Attended and/or Conducted trading card shows in Kentucky, Ohio and Florida)...

Hardback books:

KENTUCKY WILDCATS: A Story of Kentucky Football
KENTUCKY BASKETBALL'S BIG BLUE MACHINE (Award Winner)
JOE B. HALL: My Own Kentucky Home
THE WILDCAT LEGACY, a pictorial history.
ADOLPH RUPP; Kentucky's Basketball Baron (Award Winner)
THE KENTUCKY BASKETBALL VAULT

Contributor

A HISTORY OF THE SOUTHEASTERN CONFERENCE
A PICTORIAL HISTORY OF KENTUCKY (Award Winning)
THE KENTUCKY ENCYCLOPEDIA (Award Winning)

Since retiring in 1989:
1987-Present--Weekly sports column for the Cats' Pause.

1989-90--Managing editor of The Cat's Pause.

1990-91--Chief writer & production manager of Collegiate Collections, producer of college sports trading cards. (Also worked trading card shows in Kentucky, Ohio and Florida).

1996-2008--Editor, Port Orange Elks Bulletin; placed first in state. (2002), several other Top Five finishes; Port Orange Elk of the Year in 2003.

1996--Honorary member Florida Sheriff's Association. All-American Football citation.

1970'--s moonlighted as publicity director for night harness racing at Louisville Downs and Lexington's Big Red Mile. (Also P.R. director for Kentucky State Harness Racing Commission).

Member Outdoor Writers of America...former state Bait-Casting champion and president of the Kentucky Bait-Casting Association.

Enjoys reading, music, fishing, gardening, genealogy, and computers. Former Religious Sports Writer of the Year.

Scoutmaster of troops in Whitesburg, Hazard, and Lexington. Taught Sunday School in Garrett and Whitesburg. Choir member at Garrett Methodist Church. Founding elder of Hill'n Dale Christian Church, sponsor of Southland Christian, in Lexington. Former member of Board at Daytona Beach Drive-In Christian Church.

Began snow-birding in 1990, moved to South Daytona permanently in 1996.

2009—Grand Marshal, Van Lear Town Celebration.

2011—Inducted into University of Kentucky Athletic Hall of Fame.

Bookshelf Bibliographic Notes

A 22"x39" three-tiered bookshelf in my office contains more than 100 books about Kentucky basketball. This does not include UK media guides dating back to 1945.

The list begins with Greg Stanley's Before *Big Blue, University of Kentucky Press, 1995*, which chronicles the early history of organized sports at the University of Kentucky. Stanley covers the half-century (1890-1940) when football ruled the athletic department.

An autographed copy *("I hope that you enjoy every page of this book–To a real friend, Adolph F. Rupp")* of Rupp's *Championship Basketball* occupies a place of honor. It is mostly an Xs and Os publication that delves into passing, shooting, dribbling, and other intricacies of the game.

Rupp was a poetry buff, along with many other pursuits, so it was natural for him to preface the book with the following:

> *A mighty monarch in the day of old*
> *Made offer of high honors, wealth, and gold*
> *To one who should produce in form concise*
> *A precept soothing in his hours forlorn,*
> *Yet one that in his prosperous days would warn,*
> *Many the maxim sent the King, men say,*
> *The one he chose..."This too shall pass away!"*

Abraham Lincoln followed the same philosophy, Rupp said, and what was good enough for "Honest Abe" was good enough for him; however, many years after the fact Rupp still had nightmares of his "Runts" losing to Texas Western in the 1966 NCAA championship game.

In 1979, Harry Lancaster penned *Adolph Rupp As I Knew Him*, with Cawood Ledford. The only memorial thing about this paperback is Lancaster crediting Rupp with a racist remark after

UK president John W. Oswald ordered Rupp to recruit black players:

"Harry, that son of a bitch is ordering me to get some n-----s in here. What am I going to do? He's the boss."

That same year, Simon & Schuster published Frank Fitzpatrick's *And The Walls Came Tumbling Down: Kentucky, Texas Western, and the Game that Changed American Sports.* That picked up where Lancaster left off and further darkened the image of Rupp as a modern day Simon Legree.

Two valuable books in our collection are UK Professor Bert Nelli's *The Kentucky Tradition* and Tom Wallace's *The Kentucky Basketball Encyclopedia.* Both are lengthy chronicles of the Wildcat basketball program. Nelli takes a more academic approach while Wallace gives us many facts and figures that are most valuable to researchers.

Lonnie Wheeler's "Blue Yonder" is a look into the Wildcat phenomena, which Rick Pitino, in association with Dick "Hoops" Weiss, also covers in *Full Court Pressure: A Year in Kentucky Basketball.* The setting for Pitino's book is the 1991/92 season, when the Wildcats lost a heartbreaker to Duke in the NCAA Regional final.

A copy of Pitino's earlier book, *Born to Coach: A Season with the New York Knicks*, with Bill Reynolds, contains a front cover notice: "with an update that answers the question why I went to KY." It boils down to a clash of personalities between Pitino and the Knicks general manager.

Jim Host was the most productive publisher of UK books, with at least 10 to his credit. His stable of authors includes such well-known Kentucky sports personalities as Cawood Ledford and John McGill, both deceased; Billy Reed, Oscar Combs, Mike Embry and Tom Wallace. Former UK sports information directors Chris Cameron and Brooks Downing and former assistant basketball coach and former athletic directors Harry Lancaster and C.M. also contributed to Host's mixture.

Billy Reed is an award-winning journalist who has been covering sports in Kentucky since 1959. A native of Mt. Sterling, he is a 1966 graduate of Transylvania University, which awarded him a distinguished alumni award in 1980. Reed has worked for the *Lexington Herald-Leader, the Courier-Journal,* and *Sports Illustrated.* He has many works to his credit.

Cawood Ledford, legendary "Voice of the Wildcats", was working on his seventh book for Host when he died of cancer in 2001.

Tom Wallace once served as editor of *Cawood on Kentucky.* He is a former columnist for *The Cats' Pause*

Jamie H. Vaught has written four books containing interviews with players, coaches and others associated with the UK basketball program. He spent 13 years as a columnist for *The Cats' Pause* and currently works for *The Daily News March Madness* in Middlesboro. Jamie is an associate professor of accounting at Southeast Community College.

Kentucky's two major newspapers, *The Courier-Journal* and *The Herald-Leader*, have been major contributors to the list of UK publications, especially in coverage of championships won or nearly won. They are included in the following list of books on our basketball shelf:

CHAMPIONSHIP BASKETBALL, by Adolph F. Rupp, Prentice-Hall, 1948.

THE RUPP YEARS, by Tevis Laudeman, the Courier-Journal, 1972.

BASKETBALL: The Dream Game In Kentucky, by Dave Kindred, Data Courier, Inc., 1976.

KENT*UCKY BASKETBALL'S BIG BLUE MACHINE,* by Russell Rice, Strode Publishers, Huntsville, Ala., 1976.

A YEAR AT THE TOP, *by John McGill and Walt Johnson, photography* by Walt Johnson, Jim Host and Associates Inc., 1978.

BASKETBALL IN THE BLUE GRASS STATE: The Championship Teams, by Mike Embry, Leisure Press, New York, 1983.

MARCH MADNESS: The Kentucky High School Basketball Tournament, by Mike Embry, Icarus Press, South Bend, 1985.

RICK PITINO: Born to Coach, A Season with the New York Knicks, with Bill Reynolds, New American Library, New York, 1988."

ADOLPH RUPP AS I KNEW HIM, by Harry Lancaster, with Cawood Ledford. 1979.

BASKETBALL *PITINO STYLE, with Cawood Ledford,* by Chris Cameron, Host Communications, Inc., 1990.

THE MAKING OF CHAMPIONS: Kentucky Basketball 1979-1980, by Oscar Combs, Photography by Bill Straus and Allen Malott, Lexington Productions, Inc.

MACY, by Kyle Macy as told to Cawood Ledford, Lexington Productions, Inc., 1980

BIG BLUE MANIA: Kentucky Basketball 1981-82, by Oscar Combs, Lexington Productions, Inc., 1982.

FULL-COURT PRESSURE: A Year in Kentucky Basketball, by Rick Pitino, Hyperion, New York, 1992.

THE LIVES OF RILEY, by Mark Heisler, Macmillan USA, 1984 by Greg Stanley, University of Kentucky Press, 1995

THE CARR CREEK LEGACY by Don Miller. Vantage Press. 1995.

HEART OF BLUE, by Cawood Ledford, Host Communications, Inc. 1995.

THE LEGACY AND THE GLORY, Greatest moments in Kentucky Basketball History, edited by Mike Bynum, Ad Craft, 1995.

THE OFFICIAL UNIVERSITY OF KENTUCKY BASKETBALL BOOK, by Randall S. Baron and Russell Rice, Devyn Press, 1986.

UNTOUCHABLE*: THE CROWNING OF THE COMMONWEALTH*, Host Communications, Inc., 1996.

GO BIG BLUE: Relive Kentucky's Memorial 1995-96 Season, by the staff of the Lexington Herald-Leader, Lexington Herald-Leader Co., 1996.

JOURNEY TO GREATNESS: The 1995-96 Kentucky Wildcats' National Championship, edited by Francis J. Fitzgerald, Ad Craft. 1996.

A YEAR WITH THE CATS: From Breathitt County to the White House, by Dave Kindred, Jim Host & Associates Inc., 1997.

A LEGACY OF CHAMPIONS, Edited by Mike Bynum, Epic Sports, Masters Press, Indianapolis, 1997

BLUE GRIT: A Review of Kentucky's Courageous 1996-97 Season, by the staff of the Lexington Herald-Leader, the Lexington Herald Co., 1997.

COMEBACK CATS: The 1997-98 Kentucky Wildcats' Unforgettable National Championship Season, edited by Mike Bynum, from the Sports Pages of the Courier-Journal.

BLUE YONDER, by Lonnie Wheeler, Orange Fraser Press, Inc., Wilmingham, Ohio, 1998.

A DREAM COME TRUE, by Cameron Mills & Brooks Downing, Addax Publishing Group, Lenexa, Kansas, 1998.

CATS UP CLOSE: Champions of Kentucky Basketball, by Jamie H. Vaught, McClanahan Publishing House, Cutaway, Ky., 1999.

NEWTON'S LAWS, The C.M. Newton Story as told to Billy Reed, Host Communications, Inc., 2000.

BARON OF THE BLUEGRASS: Winning Words of Wisdom by and about ADOLPH Rupp, Legendary Kentucky Basketball Coach, by Mike Embry, Towle House Publishing Co., Nashville, 2000.

BASKETBALL IN THE BLUE GRASS: The Championship Teams, by Mike Embry, Leisure Press, New York, 1983.

MARCH MADNESS: The Kentucky High School Basketball Tournament, by Mike Embry., Icarus Press, South Bend, Ind. 1985.

THE KENTUCKY BASKETBALL ENC YCLOPEDIA, by Tom Wallace

100 YEARS OF KENTUCKY BASKETBALL: University of Kentucky, Publishers Mitch Barnhart (UK) & Host Communications.

KRAZY ABOUT KENTUCKY: Big Blue Hoops, by Jamie H. Vaught, Wasteland Press, Louisville, 2003

BIG BLUE: 100 Years of Kentucky Wildcats Basketball, by Michael Bradley, Sporting News, 2002.

UK 100: A CENTURY OF BASKETBALL: A commemorative publication by the Lexington Herald-Leader sports staff.

BASKETBALL CENTURY OF CHAMPIONS, by TCP staff members, edited by Darrell Bird, the Cats' Pause, 2002.

TALES FROM THE KENTUCKY HARDWOOD: A Collection of the Greatest Kentucky Basketball Stories Ever Told, by Denny Trease, Sports Publishing LLC, 2002

HEART OF A CHAMPION, By Jeff Sheppard and Tom Wallace, Addax Publishing Group, Lenexa, KS, 1998.

THE WILDCAT LEGENCY,: A Pictorial History of Kentucky Basketball, by Russell Rice, JCP Corp. of Virginia, Virginia Beach, Va., 1982.

KENTUCKY'S BASKETBALL BARON, by Russell Rice, Sagamore Publishing, Champaign, Ill., 1994. FIRST CATS: Amazing Origins of the UK Sports Tradition, by Tom Stephens, Oakleaf Publishing, Inc., 2006.

AND THE WALLS CAME TUMBLING DOWN: Kentucky, Texas Western, and the Game that Changed American Sports, by Frank Fitzpatrick 2006,

Born to Coach: A Season with the New York Knicks, by Rick Pitino, with Dick "Hoops" Weiss,

THE KENTUCKY BASKETBALL VAULT; A History of UK Basketball, by Russell Rice, Whitman Publishers, LCC, 2009.

KHSAA SWEET SIXTEEN: Boys' Tournament History and Record Book, edited by John McGill, first published in 1982.

BOUNCE BACK, by John Calipari, Simon & Schuster, 2010, 304 pages.

BEYOND A DREAM: A Mother's Courage a Family's Fight, a Son's Determination, by Mark Krebs with Dr. James Conrad Gerner, Beyond a Dream Publishing, 2010.

100 Things Wildcats Fans Should Know & Do Before They Die. [Paperback], by Ryan Clark and Joe Cox

Wildcatology Trivia Challenge: Kentucky Wildcats Basketball [Paperback] (researched by) Tom P. Rippey III (Author), Kick The Ball (Editor)

Echoes of Kentucky Basketball: The Greatest Stories Ever Told, by
Scott Strickland, Triumph Books, Tubby Smith (Foreword) [Hardcover]

Kentucky: Memorable Stories of Wildcat Basketball (Game of My Life), by Ryan Clark, Sports Publishing. [Hardcover]

The History of Kentucky Basketball (2007), D.P. Carlson (Director), Lauren Himel (Director)

100 Things...Fans Should Know, by Ryan Clark and Joe Cox, [Paperback]

Throughout my career as a newspaperman (1951–1967), a sports publicist (1967–1989), an author, and a quarter-century as a columnist for *The Cats' Pause,* I interviewed a myriad of UK athletes, past and present. My articles in TCP alone numbered more than one thousand. They were a basic research tool for this book.

Unless otherwise indicated, all pictures in this book are from University of Kentucky Media Relations, or the Russell Rice collection.

www.ingramcontent.com/pod-product-compliance
Lightning Source LLC
Chambersburg PA
CBHW060918040426
42445CB00011B/675